THE EXPLANATION OF THE CHAPTERS ON

KNOWLEDGE, RIGHTEOUSNESS & GOOD MANNERS

First Edition: 2014

ISBN: 978-1-910015-04-9

Printed and Distributed by:

Darussalam International Publications Ltd.
Leyton Business Centre
Unit-17, Etloe Road, Leyton, London, E10 7BT
Tel: 0044 208539 4885   Fax: 00442085394889
Website: www.darussalam.com
Email: info@darussalam.com

Cover design, editing and typesetting by:
Abū Fātimah Azhar Majothī
www.ihsaandesign.com

THE EXPLANATION OF THE CHAPTERS ON

KNOWLEDGE, RIGHTEOUSNESS & GOOD MANNERS

*From the Classical Collection of Hadith
Riyaadh As-Saaliheen by Imam An-Nawawi*

Explained by the Esteemed Shaykh,
and Reviver of the Sunnah,
Shaykh Muhammad Ibn Saalih Uthaymeen ﷻ

Translated and Summarised by
Taalib Ibn Tyson Al-Britaani

DARUSSALAM

GLOBAL LEADER IN ISLAMIC BOOKS

Riyadh • Jeddah • Al-Khobar • Sharjah • Lahore • London • Houston • New York

بسم الله الرحمن الرحيم

CONTENTS

AUTHOR'S BIOGRAPHY IN BRIEF[1]

HIS LINEAGE:

His name is Yahya Ibn Sharfuddeen Muree Ibn Hasan Al-Hizaammee Al-Huraanee, he was also known as Abu Zakariyyah; however he did not have a son named Zakariyyah as he did not marry.

He was given the nickname *Muhyee-ud Deen* (Reviver of the Religion); never the less he used to despise this title, and disliked being called that out of humbleness to Allah. One of the reasons why he disliked it was because Allah's Religion is continuous and need of no one but Allah to keep it alive and established.

It has been said that Imam An-Nawawi once said "I shall not forgive the one who gives me this title *Muhyee-ud Deen* (Reviver of the Religion)." In another report it is stated that he

---

[1] *Tadhkiratul Hufaaz* 4/1470-1474, page 177-180 by Imam Adh-Dhahabi. Daaru Ihyaa'ut Turaathul Arabi and for further reference on the life of Imam An-Nawawi, see our noble Shaykh Mashoor Hasan's book *Ar-Radoodu wal Ta'qibaat,* p304, *Al-Musahaha.*

said "It is impermissible for someone to nickname me *Muhyee ul-Deen.*"

HIS PLACE OF BIRTH:

He was born in Nawa the capital of Julaan in the land of Huraan in the year 631H in the month of Muharram. It is said that he was given this name Al-Nawawi by virtue of his place of birth Nawa and his place of residence was Damascus, Syria.

HIS EARLY LIFE:

He memorised the *Quran* before puberty abandoning distractions and play; his burning thirst for knowledge could not be quenched in Nawa, so his father took him at the age of 19 to seek knowledge in Damascus and he enrolled at the School of Rawaahiyyah in the year 649H.

During this time in just four and a half months he memorized the book *At-Tanbeh* authored by Abu Ishaaq Al-Sheeraaree in addition he memorized a quarter of *Al-Ibaadaat* from the book *Al-Muhadhab Fee Furoo* during the remainder of that year. He would study 12 lessons a day and when revising these lessons on his way to his classes and on his way home, it was said, that not a moment of his life was wasted except that is was in the pursuit of *Ilm*.

HIS LATER LIFE:

He taught in many institutes and from them, *Al-Madrasah Al-Iqbaaliyaah* and *Al-Fulkeeyah* and *Rukuneeyah*. He was also appointed senior instructor in the institute *Daarul Hadith Al-*

Ashraaqeeyah after Abu Shaamah Abdir Rahmaan passed away in the year 665H and continued till his own death in year 676H

HIS SHUYOOKH:

Imam An-Nawawi had many *Shuyookh* (pl. Shaykh), too many to mention but his main and primary teacher was Shaykh Ishaaq Ibn Ahmad Ibn Uthmaan Al-Magribi Al-Maqdisi.[2]

HIS STUDENTS:

Some say it was over one hundred students.

HIS WRITINGS:

Imam An-Nawawi authored many works; we will mention just a few:

- *Forty Ahaadith*
- *Sharh Sahih Muslim*
- *Sharh Sahihul Bukhari*
- *Sharh Sunnan Abee Dawood*
- *Irshaad*
- *Al-Majmoo Sharh Al-Muhadhdhab*
- *Raudhatut Taalibeen*
- *Minhaajal Taalibeen*
- *Tibyaan Fee Aadaab Hamlatil Quran*
- *Bustaan Al-Aarifeen*
- *Al-Adhkaar*

---

[2] For further reference on the names of Imam An-Nawawi's *Shuyookh* see *Al-Bidaayah wa Nihaayah* by Ibn Kathir, 13/278.

SCHOLARS WHO WROTE BIOGRAPHIES ABOUT HIM:

From the *Ulama* (Scholars) who wrote a biography about him we will mention just a few:

- *Al-Minhaajul Sawee fee Tarjamah Al-Imam An-Nawawi.*[3]
- *Tuhfatul Taalibeen Fee Tarjamah Al-Muhyyee ul Deen.*[4]
- *Munhal Al-Adhab Al-Rawee Fee Tarjamah Al-Imam An-Nawawi.*[5]
- *Tabaqaat As'Shaafi'eeyah Al-Kubrah.*[6]

HIS DEATH:

The great Imam traveled to Jerusalem after remaining in Damascus for almost 29 years, after which he returned to his home town Nawa where he became very ill in the house of his father who was looking after him. It was here that the Imam passed away in the year 676H in the month of Rajab. And this is where he was buried.

---

[3] By As-Suyooti
[4] By Ibnul Attaar
[5] By As-Sakhaawee
[6] By As-Subki

SHAYKH IBN UTHAYMEEN'S
BIOGRAPHY IN BRIEF[7]

HIS LINEAGE:

He is Abu Abdullah Muhammad Ibn Saalih Ibn Muhammad Ibn Uthaymeen Al-Wuhaybee at-Tameemee.

HIS PLACE OF BIRTH:

He was born in the city of Unaynah in the region of Qaseem region of Saudi Arabia on the 27 of the month of Ramadan on 1347H which corresponds to around 1926.

HIS EARLY LIFE:

He would recite the Quran with his maternal grandfather Abdur Rahmaan Ibn Suleiman Al-Daamigh. He then memorized the whole Quran and took a path in pursuing knowledge. He learned how to write Arabic, arithmetic and many other subjects.

---

[7] For further information about the Shaykh, refer to *Al-Jaami li'Hataaytil Alaamah Muhammad Ibn Saalihul Uthaymeen* by one of his students Waleed Ibn Ahmad Al-Hussain.

The Noble Shaykh, Abdur Rahmaan As-Sa'dee's two students Shaykh Ali As-Saalihee and Shaykh Muhammad Ibn Abdul-Azeez Al-Mutawwi took up the task of teaching the young children.

Shaykh Muhammad Ibn Abdul-Azeez taught Shaykh Ibn Uthaymeen the abridgement of Ibn Taymiyyah's *Aqeedatul Waasitiyah,* written by Shaykh As'Sadee and *Minhaajus Saalikeen fi Fiqh* by Shaykh As'Sadee; he also studied *Al-Aajurrumiyyah* and *Al-Alfiyyah.*

Under Shaykh Abdur Rahmaan Ibn Ali Awdaan, he studied the laws of inheritance and *Fiqh,* and from these who were considered his first Shaykh was Shaykh As-Sa'dee, who he stayed with for a period of time and studied with him *Tawheed, Fiqh, Usoolul Fiqh, Faraa'id, Usoolul Hadith, Nahoo, Sarf, Hadith and Tafsir.*

He also studied under His Eminence Shaykh Ibn Baz who was his second Shaykh, and with whom he studied Al-Bukhari and some of the works of Ibn Taymiyyah and some books of *Fiqh.*

HIS LATER LIFE:

In the year 1371H Ibn Uthaymeen began to teach in the *Masjid,* and when an institute opened in Riyadh he unrolled in 1372 and two years later he graduated and was given a position as a teacher at the institute in Unayzah.

He continued his studies with the College of Sharia and Shaykh As-Sa'dee until his death. Ibn Uthaymeen replaced As-Sa'dee in the main *Masjid* in Unayzah where he served as *Imam* and *Khateeb.* Ibn Uthaymeen also taught at the library in Unayzah as well as the Department of Sharia and Theology in the Qaseem branch of Muhammad Ibn Su'ood Islamic University.

The Shaykh was also a member of the senior council of eminent Scholars of Saudi Arabia. It is worth mentioning that the late Mufti Muhammad Ibn Ibraheem offered him to take the position of a judge many times, but the Shaykh excused himself

HIS SHUYOOKH:

- Shaykh Muhammad Al-Ameen Ibn Muhammad Al-Muktaar Al-Juknee Al-Shanqeeti.
- Shaykh Ali Ibn Hamid Al-Saalihee as well as those already mentioned.

HIS STUDENTS:

It is reported that there were too many to count, some say over five hundred.

HIS WRITINGS:

It has been mentioned that his works exceed 80 in number and they mostly consists of small treatises.

HIS DEATH:

The Shaykh passed away on Wednesday, the 15th of Shawwaal, 1421, corresponding to January 10th, 2001 at the age seventy four years of age.

باب العلم

THE CHAPTER ON KNOWLEDGE

TRANSLATOR'S PREFACE

Verily all praises are due to Allah. We praise Him and seek His help and forgiveness. We seek refuge with Allah from our evil souls and our wrong doings. He whom Allah guides, no one can misguide and He whom He misguides, no one can guide.

I bear witness that there is no true god except Allah alone without any partners. And I bear witness that Muhammad is His *Abd* (servant) and Messenger.

يَـٰٓأَيُّهَا ٱلَّذِينَ ءَامَنُواْ ٱتَّقُواْ ٱللَّهَ حَقَّ تُقَاتِهِۦ وَلَا تَمُوتُنَّ إِلَّا وَأَنتُم مُّسۡلِمُونَ

"O you who believe! Fear Allah as He should be feared and die not except in a state of submission." (Aali Imraan, 102)

يَـٰٓأَيُّهَا ٱلنَّاسُ ٱتَّقُواْ رَبَّكُمُ ٱلَّذِى خَلَقَكُم مِّن نَّفۡسٍ وَٰحِدَةٍ وَخَلَقَ مِنۡهَا زَوۡجَهَا وَبَثَّ مِنۡهُمَا رِجَالًا كَثِيرًا وَنِسَآءً وَٱتَّقُواْ ٱللَّهَ ٱلَّذِى تَسَآءَلُونَ بِهِۦ وَٱلۡأَرۡحَامَ إِنَّ ٱللَّهَ كَانَ عَلَيۡكُمۡ رَقِيبًا

"O mankind! Be dutiful to Your Lord Who created you from a single soul and from him created its mate, and from them both He created many men and women; and fear Allah through Whom you demand your mutual rights and do not sever the relations of the wombs (Kinship) Indeed, Allah is Ever an All-Watcher over you." (An-Nisaa, 1)

يَـٰٓأَيُّهَا ٱلَّذِينَ ءَامَنُواْ ٱتَّقُواْ ٱللَّهَ وَقُولُواْ قَوْلاً سَدِيدًا • يُصْلِحْ لَكُمْ أَعْمَـٰلَكُمْ وَيَغْفِرْ لَكُمْ ذُنُوبَكُمْ وَمَن يُطِعِ ٱللَّهَ وَرَسُولَهُۥ فَقَدْ فَازَ فَوْزًا عَظِيمًا

"O you who believe! Fear Allah and say just words. He will direct you to do good deeds and forgive you your sins. He who obeys Allah and His Messenger have certainly achieved a great victory." (Al-Ahzaab, 70-71)

Verily, the best speech is Allah's Speech and the best of guidance is Muhammad's guidance, and the worst matters (in creed or worship) are those innovated (by the people), for every innovated matter is a Bidah (prohibited innovation), and every Bidah is an act of misguidance that (whoever initiated it) will reside in the Fire.[8]

It gives me great honour to be able to translate this chapter, the Chapter of Knowledge from one of Imam An-Nawawi's most famous books, *Riyaadus Saliheen,* along with

---

[8] Reported by Muslim. A full discussion of the various reports of this sermon can be found in Shaykh Al-Albaani's booklet "*Khutba'tul'Haajah,*" published by Al-Maktabul Islaamee Beirut.

the explanation of the esteemed Scholar Shaykh Ibn Uthaymeen.

Imam An-Nawawi's purpose for writing such an outstanding book was to encourage others to do good. So for this reason I have specifically chosen this chapter regarding *Ilm* [9](knowledge), in the hope of encouraging my brothers and sisters wherever they may be and in whatever circumstances they find themselves in, to not give up the pursuit of seeking *Ilm*. Especially in the time we are living in whereby the desire for seeking *Ilm* has, with deep regret, decreased greatly. So I hope that translating Shaykh Ibn Uthaymeen's explanation of the chapter of *Ilm*, will re-light the flame that many of us once had burning in us and awaken us from our prolonged sleeplessness and prevent us from wasting our time and spend more of it seeking knowledge as well as practicing it, as the *Salaf* used to say:

> *"Knowledge calls for action, so either the call is answered or it will take off."* [10]

So we must return to seeking knowledge if we are not already doing that and remember its great virtues, for by not doing so we are preventing ourselves from much good; and the proof for my claim is as Al-Hasan Al-Basri said:

---

[9] *Ilm* (knowledge) is more specific than (merely) knowing things - what is intended by this, in the Sharia, is knowledge of the Quran which was revealed to the Prophet ﷺ. Al-Bayhaqee said: *"The meaning of Ilm is knowledge of the Quran and the Sunnah, and the statements of the Companions and their followers and what they were upon."*

[10] *Muftaaru daarus Sa'aadah* 1-511 /519 this is also the statement of Ali; see *Al-Jaami* by Al-Khateeb and *Dhim Man laa Ya'mal bi Ilmihi* by Ibn Asaakir and *Lisaanul Mizaan* 4-26/27 by Ibn Hajar.

"That I learn one chapter pertaining to Ilm, then teach it to a Muslim, is better to me than having the whole world and spending it in Allah's cause."[11]

Regarding the great virtue of seeking *Ilm* is the statement of the *Taabi'* Mutraf Ibn Abdullah:

"Ilm (knowledge) is better and more virtuous than worship! Do you not see the monks who devote their whole night to pray, then sleep, but wake up only to associate partners with Allah?"[12]

Also the Prophets said:

The excellence of knowledge is greater than optional actions and the best of your religion is piety.[13]

So brothers and sisters this is the way of our *Salaf! Ilm* meant a lot to them and seeking it, and they considered it the best way to gain closeness to Allah ﷻ and this is backed by the statement of Az-Zuhri who said:

"Allah is not worshipped with anything better than with Ilm."[14]

So the *Salaf's* methodology should strictly be followed regarding worshipping Allah, as their way has the stamp of approval.

Sufyaan Ath-Thawree said:

---

[11] *Al-Fiqhi wal Mutafiqhi,* 1/102.
[12] *Jaami Bayaanul Ilm,* 1/119.
[13] *At-Targheeb wat Tarheeb* 65 and authenticated by Shaykh Al-Albaani.
[14] *Kitaabul Fiqihi* 1/103.

"No act of worship is greater than seeking Ilm, if ones intentions are correct." [15]

Also Ibnul Mubarak said:
"I know of nothing greater than seeking Ilm for the one who intends Allah." [16]

It was once asked to Ibnul Mubarak: "If you knew you had one day left to live what would you spend that last day doing?" He replied:
"I would spend it (that last day) teaching the people." [17]

So in short, know, may Allah have mercy upon you! Take to the path of seeking *Ilm*, as this is something we lack greatly. Imam Ash-Shaafi said:
"Seeking Ilm is better than any optional prayers." [18]

And as it was said by a poet:
"So know, if you seek Ilm, then it is like you are in pursuit of the most precious object, so beware of what you are in pursuit of! So, if you are aware of this fact, then focus your heart on nothing but the pursuit of seeking Ilm." [19]

---

[15] *Jaami Bayaanul Ilm* 1/119-120.
[16] *Al-Madkhal Illas Sunnul Kubarah* 2/44-45.
[17] Ibid.
[18] *Al-Madkhal* 2/45 and *Jaami' Bayaanul Ilm* 1/123.
[19] *Al-Jawaa'harul Madiyatul fee Tabaqaatul Hanafiyah* 3/324.

I ask Allah ﷻ to accept this translation from me and to make it of great benefit to the reader; indeed, He is able to do all things.

Taalib Tyson
Jordan Amman
July 2014 / Ramadaan 1435

[CHAPTER] THE VIRTUES OF KNOWLEDGE WHICH IS LEARNT AND TAUGHT FOR THE SAKE OF ALLAH

Allah the Exalted says in the Quran:

$$وَقُل رَّبِّ زِدْنِي عِلْمًا$$

"And say: My Lord! Increase me in knowledge."
(Taha, 114)

Allah the Exalted also says:

$$هَلْ يَسْتَوِى ٱلَّذِينَ يَعْلَمُونَ وَٱلَّذِينَ لَا يَعْلَمُونَ$$

"Are those who know equal to those who know not."
(Az-Zumar, 9)

Allah the Exalted also says:

$$يَرْفَعِ ٱللَّهُ ٱلَّذِينَ ءَامَنُوا۟ مِنكُمْ وَٱلَّذِينَ أُوتُوا۟ ٱلْعِلْمَ دَرَجَٰتٍ$$

"Allah will raise in degree those of you who believe, and those who have been granted knowledge."
(Al-Mujaadilah, 11)

Allah the Exalted also says:

$$إِنَّمَا يَخْشَى ٱللَّهَ مِنْ عِبَادِهِ ٱلْعُلَمَٰٓؤُا۟$$

"It is only those who have knowledge among His slaves that fear Allah." (Al-Faatir, 28)

[EXPLANATION OF CHAPTER HEADING AND SUPPORTING VERSES]

The author Imam An-Nawawi mentions in this chapter the virtues of knowledge which is learnt and taught for the sake of Allah the Exalted, and what the author intends by the term *Ilm* (knowledge) is knowledge of the Quran and the Sunnah of the Prophet 鷺, its virtue and the reward obtained by seeking it and it exalting the possessors of it, who are the inheritors of the Prophets.

And *Ilm* is connected to Islamic law, namely the *Aqeedah* (the fundamental beliefs of Islam and rejection of false concepts), and how to implement it. And what is not intended by the meaning of knowledge here, is knowledge regarding worldly matters like accounting or engineering and the likes.

So what is meant by *Ilm* like we said, is what pertains to the correct Islamic fundamentals and concepts, this is the *Ilm* we mean as Allah the Exalted rewards the seeker for obtaining such *Ilm* (knowledge), practicing and propagating it.

So, *Ilm* which is sought is a type of striving (jihad), a striving in the way of Allah! With it, the foundations and struggling in Allah's way are built. Because without *Ilm*, it is impossible for one to implement what is required of him in the correct way, so due to this Allah the Exalted says in the Quran:

وَمَا كَانَ ٱلْمُؤْمِنُونَ لِيَنفِرُواْ كَآفَّةً فَلَوْلَا نَفَرَ مِن كُلِّ فِرْقَةٍ مِّنْهُمْ طَآئِفَةٌ لِّيَتَفَقَّهُواْ فِى ٱلدِّينِ وَلِيُنذِرُواْ قَوْمَهُمْ إِذَا رَجَعُوٓاْ إِلَيْهِمْ لَعَلَّهُمْ يَحْذَرُونَ

"And it is not (proper) for the believers to go out to fight (*Jihaad*) all together. Of every troop of them, a party only should go forth, that they (who are left behind) may get instructions in (Islamic) religion, and that they may warn their people when they return to them, so that they may beware (of evil). (At-Tawbah, 122)

So what is meant here is: not every individual should participate in jihad, rather one group should go forth and one group remain behind, that group remaining behind are those seeking Islamic knowledge, so that when the group that has gone forth to fight return, those who remained behind seeking *Ilm* can warn, advice or consult them upon their return.

So Allah the Exalted put both groups on the same footing! And what we mean is, that those who remained behind seeking *Ilm* are equivalent to those who went out in the way of Allah; remaining behind seeking *Ilm* was equal to actually fighting jihad on the battle field.

Seeking *Ilm* precedes jihad and is greater! Why? The reason is, it is not possible for a fighter to fight, a person to pray, a person to pay zakat, to fast, to perform Hajj or Umrah, eat and drink or sleep or wake up except that he does so based upon *Ilm*!

So the basis of all things is learning before acting; because of this the Prophet said in a *Hadith*:
"*Whoever Allah wants good for, He gives him an understanding of the Deen (religion).*"

So there is no difference between a mujaahid (one who fights in the cause of Allah) and a talibul ilm (seeker of knowledge) - one who seeks *Ilm* from the books of the people of knowledge and propagates it; and why we say this, is because both strive to make Allah's Religion superior and they both have the intention of doing these things for Allah's sake.

So those who know Imam An-Nawawi's book *Riyaadus Saaliheen* know that the chapter before this chapter (on knowledge) is the chapter of jihad. Why? To show you that this chapter is equal and the same, rather some *Ulama* (Scholars), may Allah may mercy upon them, have said, seeking *Ilm* is more virtuous than jihad.

And that which is correct is, jihad is more preferable for some and for some people seeking *Ilm* is preferable. So we say if a person is fit and strong and ready for defending Islam, then in that case jihad in his case would be better for him.

But on the other hand now, if the person finds his self weak, not brave, but he has strong memory and understands thing quickly, then in his case, seeking *Ilm* is preferable.

Now let's say that if both things were present in one person, his strong, brave, sharp memory and comprehension of things is very strong, then the *Ulama,* may Allah have mercy upon them, say in this case he should seek *Ilm*. Again we say why? The reason why is that he will be able to spread Islam and benefit the people who are in great need of guidance, at that time he propagates this knowledge or after he dies leaving this *Ilm* to benefit those who come after him. How this *Ilm* benefits him after his death is explained in the following *Hadith*; the Prophet ﷺ said:

> *"When a man dies, his deeds come to an end except for three things: Sadaqah Jaariyah (ceaseless charity); a knowledge which is beneficial, or a virtuous descendant who prays for him (for the deceased)."*

So all are in need of *Ilm*, the Prophets and other than them and for this reason Allah the Exalted says to Prophet Muhammad in the Quran:

$$وَقُل رَّبِّ زِدْنِي عِلْمًا$$

"And say: My Lord! Increase me in knowledge." (Taha, 114)

The full verse reads:

$$فَتَعَٰلَى ٱللَّهُ ٱلْمَلِكُ ٱلْحَقُّ ۗ وَلَا تَعْجَلْ بِٱلْقُرْءَانِ مِن قَبْلِ أَن يُقْضَىٰٓ إِلَيْكَ وَحْيُهُۥ ۖ وَقُل رَّبِّ زِدْنِي عِلْمًا$$

"And be not in haste (O Muhammad) with the Quran before its revelation is complete to you; and say: 'My Lord! Increase me in knowledge.'"

Even the Messengers were all in great need of *Ilm* and an increase in it, and they used to ask Allah the Exalted for an increase in it. So if this was their case, that they would ask Allah for an increase in knowledge due to the great need and desire for an increase in it, what then would be the case of those who are in a lesser position than them, would they not then be in an even greater need for *Ilm*!?

So it is only appropriate for the seeker of knowledge to constantly ask the Exalted for an increase in his knowledge, but, I must point out that, it is incumbent upon the seeker of knowledge to ask Allah for an increase in *Ilm* but at the same time he should take the appropriate steps in inquiring it! And what we mean by this is that it would not be a wise action to be saying to Allah increase my *Ilm* but he does not go out in pursuit of it, this would be wrong!

Again would this be a wise thing, that a person asks Allah to give him offspring, but avoids marriage? No it would be unwise. How, if he does not marry, will he produce children! So in short, if you are going to ask Allah for your needs to be met, take the precautions or strive as much as you can in obtaining that sought-after subject. Because Allah is Al-Hakeem (All-Wise) and He has made the seeking after the sought item a way of and means of obtainment. So this verse:

$$وَقُل رَّبِّ زِدْنِي عِلْمًا$$

"And say: My Lord! Increase me in knowledge." (Taha, 114)

This is a proof confirming the lofty status of *Ilm*. If, on the other hand, having wealth had a loftier status, Allah would have advised the Prophet ﷺ to say "O my Lord! Increase me in wealth," which is not the case, rather "Increase me in *Ilm*." Allah says to the Prophet ﷺ regarding the *Dunya* (the life of this world):

وَلَا تَمُدَّنَّ عَيْنَيْكَ إِلَىٰ مَا مَتَّعْنَا بِهِۦٓ أَزْوَٰجًا مِّنْهُمْ زَهْرَةَ ٱلْحَيَوٰةِ ٱلدُّنْيَا

لِنَفْتِنَهُمْ فِيهِ ۚ وَرِزْقُ رَبِّكَ خَيْرٌ وَأَبْقَىٰ

"And strain not your eyes in longing for the things We have given for enjoinment to various groups of them (polytheist and disbelievers in the Oneness of Allah), the splendor of the life of this world that We may test them thereby. But the provisions (good deeds in the Hereafter) of your Lord is better and more lasting." (Taha, 131)

So we ask the Exalted to grant us beneficial *Ilm* and righteous good deeds, and enable us to call to Your Religion upon clear insight.

As for the remaining verses of this chapter, Allah the Exalted says:

هَلْ يَسْتَوِى ٱلَّذِينَ يَعْلَمُونَ وَٱلَّذِينَ لَا يَعْلَمُونَ

"Are those who know equal to those who know not." (Az-Zumar, 9)

Allah the Exalted also says:

يَرْفَعِ ٱللَّهُ ٱلَّذِينَ ءَامَنُوا۟ مِنكُمْ وَٱلَّذِينَ أُوتُوا۟ ٱلْعِلْمَ دَرَجَٰتٍ

"Allah will raise in degree those of you who believe, and those who have been granted knowledge." (Al-Mujaadilah, 11)

The *Ulama* have said that *Ilm* is divided into two categories:
  1. Individual duty

2. Collective duty

Regarding the first division, the individual duty, then it is *Ilm* that is required upon every Muslim to know. As for the second division, then it is a collective duty, and that is a requirement upon some Muslims but not all, and what we mean by this is that if some Muslims obtain this knowledge the rest are exempt from requiring it or the obligation is lifted from them all.

Regarding this second division, is has a subdivision connected to it which we will explain. And that is, if some seek *Ilm*, it is only *Sunnah* or recommended upon the rest of the Muslims.

So we will shed a little more light briefly upon the individual duty, and it is that knowledge with regards to those things in Islam that are an obligation upon all the Muslims to know and learn; i.e. regarding *Tawheed*, its clarification, what negates it, matters regarding *Shirk* (polytheism), its major or minor aspects, its manifest as well as it hidden aspects, all this is required (*waajib*) to learn upon every follower of Islam.

Knowing Allah, His Oneness and what is related to it, similarly regarding knowing about the prayer, because prayer is a must upon every individual as long as he or she has a sound mind. And the same goes for (*Wudu*) purification and other than that so that the slave worships Allah upon insight.

The same regarding zakat and its rules and regulations and who it is upon to pay it and so forth. But in saying this we must say that zakat is only *waajib* upon those who are in possession of things that zakat is required for.

And the same goes for fasting, which is not required upon every Muslim to know its rules and regulations, who fasting is *Waaajib* upon and not, what nullifies it, etc. and the same goes for *Hajj*, which in not a must upon every Muslim.

With great regret many people have become ignorant regarding Islam! They are unaware of many things which are obliged upon them, and we just mentioned *Hajj*, but in saying this, this act is one of the acts many people make many mistakes when preforming it and we are constantly asked questions regarding that and have talked with many people who have performed *Hajj* and we have discovered many of them have fallen into many no-go areas.

And again, regarding trading, buying and selling, knowing the rules and regulation regarding it is only a must to know upon those who are in trade or those who intend to go into trade, so as to be upon clear insight regarding it. So as for Allah the Exalted's statement:

هَلْ يَسْتَوِى ٱلَّذِينَ يَعْلَمُونَ وَٱلَّذِينَ لَا يَعْلَمُونَ

"Are those who know equal to those who know not."
(Az-Zumar, 9)

This verse shows the virtue of *Ilm*. It is in the form of a question, and what we mean is that, Allah is posing a form of a challenge to the reader, so it is like Allah is saying to the reader: show me someone who will say those who do not know are equal to those who know!

So the challenge would certainly not be met! And no one will be able produce someone who could, not even in worldly affairs are people on the same footing; no they fluctuate! Allah the Exalted also says:

يَرْفَعِ ٱللَّهُ ٱلَّذِينَ ءَامَنُواْ مِنكُمْ وَٱلَّذِينَ أُوتُواْ ٱلْعِلْمَ دَرَجَٰتٍ

"Allah will raise in degree those of you who believe, and those who have been granted knowledge." (Al-Mujaadilah, 11)

This verse also shows the loftiness of *Ilm*:

يَٰٓأَيُّهَا ٱلَّذِينَ ءَامَنُوٓاْ إِذَا قِيلَ لَكُمْ تَفَسَّحُواْ فِي ٱلْمَجَٰلِسِ فَٱفْسَحُواْ

يَفْسَحِ ٱللَّهُ لَكُمْ ۖ وَإِذَا قِيلَ ٱنشُزُواْ فَٱنشُزُواْ

"O you who believe! When you are told to make room in assemblies, (spread out and) make room. Allah will give you (ample) room (from His Mercy). And when you are told to rise up (for prayer, jihad, or for any other good deed) rise up." (Al-Mujaadilah 11)

Meaning stand up, raise up. Allah also says:

إِذَا قِيلَ لَكُمْ تَفَسَّحُواْ فِي ٱلْمَجَٰلِسِ فَٱفْسَحُواْ يَفْسَحِ ٱللَّهُ لَكُمْ

"When you are told to make room in assemblies, (spread out and) make room. Allah will give you (ample) room (from His Mercy)." (Al-Mujaadilah, 11)

So if a person enters a full gathering of people sitting and there is little space they should make room, and what is meant is,

Allah will give them ample room from His Mercy in their affairs. Because the origin of the matters is that a man is compensated for what good he does. Whoever deals with his brother on a good footing Allah the Exalted deals with him on an equal footing.

If you simplify your brother's affairs, Allah simplifies your affairs, if you remove one of your brother's worldly troubles, Allah in turn removes one of your troubles on the Day of Judgment, so in short Allah is in the service of His servant as long as His servant is in the service of his brother in faith. Allah the Exalted goes on to say:

$$\text{يَفْسَحِ ٱللَّهُ لَكُمْ ۖ وَإِذَا قِيلَ ٱنشُزُواْ فَٱنشُزُواْ}$$

"Allah will give you (ample) room (from His Mercy). And when you are told to rise up (for prayer, *Jihaad*, or for any other good deed) rise up."

This means: stand up if you are told to stand, and what we mean by this is, and this is proof, it is not considered disrespectful to tell a gather of people "may everyone leave now, may Allah bless you all."

Such a saying is not deemed bad mannered, and one should not feel by this embarrassed by such words. And if what we are saying needs further explaining then what we mean is, if you are invited to someone's household, be it for whatever reason, it is not befitting to prolong one's stay at that location. Why? It may be that the one who has invited you to that location, after you may have served your purpose there, might have some important matters he needs to tend to, and it might be the case that he is shy to ask you to leave in order for him to attend to those matters.

So it is not frowned upon and to be looked at as strange if one is told, or a gathering is told, that they should kindly leave. And Allah the Exalted mentions this in the Quran when this happened to the Prophet ﷺ after he had invited some Companions to his house for a meal and they prolonged their stay there; Allah says:

$$إِنَّ ذَٰلِكُمْ كَانَ يُؤْذِى ٱلنَّبِىَّ فَيَسْتَحْىِۦ مِنكُمْ ۖ وَٱللَّهُ لَا يَسْتَحْىِۦ مِنَ ٱلْحَقِّ$$

"Verily such (behavior) annoys the Prophet, and he is shy of (asking) you (to go), but Allah is not shy of (telling you) the truth." (Al-Ahzaab, 53)

The story goes that the Prophet ﷺ invited his Companions to his house for a meal, when they had finished their meal they remained at his house after their meal and prolonged their stay which annoyed him greatly and he was awfully shy to ask them to leave, but on the other hand Allah the Exalted does not feel shy from explaining the truth to you, so He (Allah) says:

$$وَإِذَا قِيلَ ٱنشُزُوا۟ فَٱنشُزُوا۟$$

"And when you are told to rise up (for prayer, *Jihaad*, or for any other good deed) rise up."

Also if you go to someone's house and he opens his door to you and says, "please come back at another time as I am busy now and am unable to invite you in," then this saying to you is acceptable and not frowned upon, as Allah the Exalted says in the Quran:

وَإِن قِيلَ لَكُمُ ٱرْجِعُوا۟ فَٱرْجِعُوا۟ هُوَ أَزْكَىٰ لَكُمْ

"And if you asked to go back, then go back, for it is purer for you." (Al-Noor, 28)

With regret, there are some people who, if it is said to them "please come later as I am a bit busy at the moment," it annoys and angers them! But the Exalted says:

هُوَ أَزْكَىٰ لَكُمْ

"It is purer for you."

So, it is better for you to return as Allah says it is a means for you to be purified. Allah the Exalted says:

يَرْفَعِ ٱللَّهُ ٱلَّذِينَ ءَامَنُوا۟ مِنكُمْ وَٱلَّذِينَ أُوتُوا۟ ٱلْعِلْمَ دَرَجَٰتٍ

"Allah will raise in degree those of you who believe, and those who have been granted knowledge." (Al-Mujaadilah, 11)

Here, Allah ﷻ does not define or clarify His meaning of "degree"; He does not elaborate what degree means! Why? We say this degree all depends on the following: upon one's strength of his *Emaan* (faith) and the level of his *Ilm*, so the more firmer his *Emaan* is and the more his *Ilm* is, the more his degree will be raised.

So dear reader, the more you increase in both (*Emaan* and *Ilm*), the higher Allah the Exalted elevates you. So strive to your upmost limit in pursuing and acquiring *Ilm*, because Allah has said:

$$يَرۡفَعِ ٱللَّهُ ٱلَّذِينَ ءَامَنُواْ مِنكُمۡ وَٱلَّذِينَ أُوتُواْ ٱلۡعِلۡمَ دَرَجَٰتٍۚ$$

"Allah will raise in degree those of you who believe, and those who have been granted knowledge." (Al-Mujaadilah, 11)

May Allah raise us and help us in His remembrance, showing Him thankfulness and being more subservient to Him as those who fear Him.

Then the author mentions this last Verse:

$$إِنَّمَا يَخۡشَى ٱللَّهَ مِنۡ عِبَادِهِ ٱلۡعُلَمَٰٓؤُاْۗ$$

"It is only those who have knowledge among His slaves that fear Allah." (Al-Faatir, 28)

Regarding the word "fear" (*al-khasheyah*), it is associated with glorification, esteem or honour, veneration, and is somewhat different from fear related to terror, fright, and being scared, because ever type of fear is veneration but not every type of veneration is fear. Let me give you an example:

A man might fear a lion, but at the same time this does not necessarily mean he venerates or glorifies it. The man fears it with the type of fear which contains fright, terror, being scared. Allah says in the Quran:

$$فَلَا تَخۡشَوۡهُمۡ وَٱخۡشَوۡنِ$$

"So fear them not, but fear Me." (Al-Baqarah, 150)

So in summary, who are those rightfully entitled to be possessors of such fear or *al-khasheyah?* They are none but the people of knowledge (the *Ulama*)! The *Ulama* are those who understand Allah the Exalted, know Him, His Names, His Attributes, His descriptions, they know His Divine Rule, Authority and Judgments, and that Allah the Exalted is complete in every fact and matter and devoid of any deficiency or lacking or incompleteness in any way, shape or form, in all matters related to Him.

So this is what is intended by this word fear! This is also proof of the great and lofty status of *Ilm* (knowledge). There is no doubt that *Ilm* is from the reason to obtain *al-khasheyah* (veneration and fear).

So, if Allah the Exalted bestows and blesses a person with fear, He protects him from falling into wrongdoing and sin! Meaning, if the slave does fall into sin, he immediately repents and turns to Allah 🕌 in forgiveness; this is the definition of fear.

[Hadith: 1377]

Mu'awiyah ⬦ reported the Messenger of Allah ﷺ said:

وَعَنْ مُعَاوِيةَ ﵁ قال : قَال رسُولُ اللَّهِ ﷺ: « مَنْ يُرِد اللَّه بِه خيْراً يُفَقِّهْهُ في الدِّينِ » متفقٌ عليه.

"When Allah wishes good for someone, He bestows upon him the understanding of the Deen." [Agreed upon by Al-Bukhari and Muslim]

[Hadith: 1378]

Ibn Mas'ud ⬦ reported the Messenger of Allah ﷺ said:

وعَنْ ابنِ مسْعُودٍ ﵁ قال : قَال رسُولُ اللَّهِ ﷺ: « لا حَسَد إلاَّ في اثْنَتَيْنِ : رَجُلٌ آتَاهُ اللَّه مَالاً فسَلَّطهُ عَلى هلَكَتِه في الحَقِّ ، ورَجُلٌ آتَاهُ اللَّه الحِكْمَةَ فهُوَ يَقْضِي بِهَا، وَيُعَلِّمُهَا » مُتَّفقٌ عَلَيهِ.

"Envy is not permitted except in two cases: A man whom Allah gives wealth, and he disposes of it rightfully, and a man to whom Allah gives knowledge which he applies and teaches it." [Agreed upon by Al-Bukhari and Muslim]

[EXPLANATION OF HADITH 1377]

So the author (Imam An-Nawawi) after mentioning the aforementioned verses of the Quran, brings the narration of Mu'awiyah ibn Abee Sufyaan where in the Messenger of Allah ﷺ said:

> *"When Allah wishes good for someone, He bestows upon him the understanding of the Deen."*

So Allah the Exalted at times decrees good, and at times bad, for His Creation, but (in reality) all His decrees are good! And what we mean by this is that Allah is conscious of what every person wishes, or He fully knows what one's heart yearns for, be it good or bad, so based on this Allah the Exalted grants or makes successful or enables prosperity for this person depending on his aspiration for good or evil; therefore if an individual aspires to evil in his heart, Allah the Exalted deserts and abandons him, and Allah's refuge is sought! Allah the Exalted says regarding this:

$$ فَلَمَّا زَاغُوٓاْ أَزَاغَ ٱللَّهُ قُلُوبَهُمۡ $$

"So when they (the people of Musa) turned away (from the Path of Allah), Allah turned their hearts away (from the Right Path)." (As-Saff, 5)

So, their hearts longed for evil and desired it greatly, Allah the Exalted led them astray due to what they longed for and desired. But on the other hand those whose hearts incline to good and desire it and yearn for it, Allah graces them and makes them prosper and successful.

So if Allah sees the slave's heart incline towards righteousness and doing good, He grants him an understanding of the *Deen,* and this understanding He grants him is unmatchable with that which He grants any other individual. So this, dear reader, is clear proof that one should immerse all his efforts and strive his hardest to his up-most in pursuing seeking *Ilm,* because if Allah the Exalted sees His slave traversing a path in the pursuit of *Ilm,* then He paves the way for this individual and facilitates and opens up for him the doors of comprehension.

Bear in mind, dear reader, if you see Allah granting you this good: this comprehension of His *Deen,* waste not a moment of any of your efforts except that it is in seeking *Ilm.* But, may Allah grant you good, remember: the main pursuit is not just in acquiring *Ilm.* No! Rather it is learning then acting upon it!

The *Salaf* used to warn the people about there being an increase among them of mere narrators and few scholars; Ibn Mas'ood said:

"How will it be! When your Scholars decrease and (mere) narrators increase!"

So we have pointed out that, if a person learns something but does not put what he has learnt into practice this is an indication that he has not been given an understanding of the *Deen.*

It could be the case that the person has memorized the biggest volume of books, be it volume after volume of fiqh, even if what he has read he fully understands, but if he does

39

not put that *Ilm* into practice then he does not deserve to be given the title of one who comprehends Allah's *Deen*.

The title he is to be given is merely a narrator or none other than a reciter. Because as we said, it is seeking *Ilm* firstly then putting it into practice. So in short, whoever seeks *Ilm*, then practices it, has been given a true understanding of Allah's *Deen*. We will give you an example to summarize up what we have said: In the Quran, the people of Prophet Shu'ayb ﷺ said to him:

$$مَا نَفْقَهُ كَثِيرًا مِّمَّا تَقُولُ$$

"We do not understand much of what you say." (Hood, 91)

What is meant by their statement? Allah prohibited them from understanding righteousness or from knowing good, and that was because Allah knew what was in their hearts pertaining to evil. So we ask Allah ﷻ to make us of those who pursue the path of *Ilm* and put it into practice, understand it and teach it.

[EXPLANATION OF HADITH 1378]

Ibn Mas'ood ﷺ reported that the Prophet ﷺ said:

"Envy is not permitted except in two cases: A man whom Allah gives wealth, and he disposes of it rightfully, and a man to whom Allah gives knowledge which he applies and teaches it."

Regarding the envy mentioned in this narration, then generally envy is forbidden and counted as one of the major sins. And if we define envy, we say that it is to dislike what Allah has bestowed upon a person from His bounties.

For example, Allah the Exalted enriches an individual with wealth, so an envier envies this, and says: "I wish Allah never gave so-and-so, such-and-such wealth," or say Allah the Exalted gives a person understanding of the *Deen*, and the envier wishes Allah never granted such *Ilm* to this individual, or Allah bestows righteous offspring to one of His slaves and this envier wishes Allah never bestowed upon so-and-so righteous offspring and so forth; such envy is counted from the major sins. Envy is a trait of the Jews; Allah the Exalted says in the Quran:

أَمْ يَحْسُدُونَ ٱلنَّاسَ عَلَىٰ مَآ ءَاتَىٰهُمُ ٱللَّهُ مِن فَضْلِهِۦ

"Or do they envy men (Muhammad and his followers) for what Allah has given them from His Bounty." (An-Nisaa', 54)

Also, the Exalted says:

وَدَّ كَثِيرٌ مِّنْ أَهْلِ ٱلْكِتَٰبِ لَوْ يَرُدُّونَكُم مِّنْ بَعْدِ إِيمَٰنِكُمْ كُفَّارًا حَسَدًا مِّنْ عِندِ أَنفُسِهِم مِّنْ بَعْدِ مَا تَبَيَّنَ لَهُمُ ٱلْحَقُّ

"Many of the people of the Scripture (Jews and Christians) wish that if they could turn you away as disbelievers after you have believed, out of envy from their own selves, even, after the truth (that Muhammad is the Messenger) has become manifest unto them." (Al-Baqarah, 109)

41

The second type of envy is jealousy and it is the type that one harbors jealous or hostility towards someone who has been favoured by Allah with wealth, *Ilm*, off-spring, honour or prestige or the like.

The essence here that we are going to clarify is regarding envy in the two following matters: firstly, regarding *Ilm*, i.e. beneficial knowledge and this is what is intended in the narration we are explaining at hand which is the statement of the Prophet ﷺ:

> *"A man to whom Allah gives knowledge which he applies and teaches it."*

So, if Allah the Exalted bestows *Ilm* to a person, and with this blessing the person propagates it among the people so as to benefit and guide them, be he an Islamic judge or otherwise, as well as himself applying this *Ilm* and living by it, then this is what one can long for, this is what one can be jealous over.

Why can one be jealous over one who has this excellence bounty? Because *Ilm* is more virtuous and excellent than wealth, and the reason is, because one guides the people to do righteous good deeds. Its excellence also is that when a person propagates this *Ilm*, say, by the media - through tapes or by authoring books and the like, when the propagator of this *Ilm* dies, we know his deeds will come to an end, but all that he left and propagated will be a means for the people to benefit from and be guided. As such, the person will be rewarded for such *Ilm* after his death until the Day of Resurrection. So whatever the people benefit from, it will be of great benefit to him in the next life. The more the *Ilm* helps the people the more this person obtains greater reward from Allah ﷻ, and this highlights as well the outstanding virtue and lofty status of knowledge.

Allah the Exalted aids the slave as long as the slave is in aid of his brother, and there is no doubt that if you are teaching the people their religion, there is no doubt that is aiding them in a great way, so by this Allah the Exalted will increase your knowledge due to the fact you are of a great service; in spreading your *Ilm*, Allah helps you. And it is a fact that the more you teach the people the more your knowledge will increase.

So do not put yourself forward to teach the people before you are fully qualified and become of those rightfully sanctioned to educate the people. The reason why we say this is because if one is not fully qualified and ready to teach the people he will end up misleading them!

Either one of the two following things could occur: he could propagate falsehood deeming it to be guidance! Or, secondly, it could be the case that he is asked about a ruling and give a misleading verdict. In short, remember *Ilm* is the greatest blessing Allah bestowed upon man after Islam and *Emaan* (faith), and this is why the Prophet ﷺ said:

"*A man to whom Allah gives knowledge which he applies and teaches it.*"

As for the statement of the Prophet ﷺ:

"*A man whom Allah gives wealth, and he disposes of it rightfully.*"

This person generously gives his wealth away in the cause of Allah seeking His pleasure, not wasting it, nor using it for nonsense, rather he uses it to benefit the people in a great way, this is the one who is envied.

So, we do not envy someone who has been given great wealth but is stingy! Why? Because his wealth is of no avail to anyone but himself. Such a person we pity, because on Judgment Day he will be questioned as to how he obtained such wealth, how he spent it and how he used it.

If we see an individual using his wealth in nothing but the way of Allah for His pleasure, such a person we say *"Maa shaa' Allah"* to them; one could be jealous and envious of this type of person. But if a person uses his wealth for his own pleasures such as buying trivial decor (such as for the house), fast sports car, then such a person has little to be envied for. Rather we say they are going overboard in spending wealth and also wasting it; and Allah loves not those who waste wealth.

Also we do not envy those whose wealth is used for neither the benefit of the peoples' worldly activities or spiritual matters, because with great regret many people just play around with their wealth, so in this case we don't envy them, but rather those who are to be envied are as we have mentioned as this is what the *Deen* permits.

So in short this what we have mentioned to you shows the lofty status of *Ilm*, and those who Allah the Exalted has enriched with it, and propagate it such that it benefits the people as well as themselves; so out of the two mentioned in this *Hadith*, the person who has a higher rank is certainly the one who has been given *Ilm*, so we ask Allah the Exalted to bestow upon us beneficial knowledge and righteous actions.

[Hadith 1379]

Abu Musa ﷺ reported the Prophet ﷺ said:

وعَنْ أبي مُوسى ﷺ قال : قَالَ النبي ﷺ: « مَثَلُ مَا بعَثَني الله بِهِ مِنَ الهُدى
والْعِلْمِ كَمَثَلِ غَيْثٍ أصاب أرْضاً ، فَكَانَتْ مِنْهَا طَائفَةٌ طَيّبةٌ قَبِلَتِ الماءَ فَأَنْبَتَتِ
الْكَلأ ، وَالْعُشْب الْكَثِيرَ ، وَكَانَ مِنْهَا أجَادِبُ أمسَكتِ الماءَ ، فَنَفَعَ الله بِهَا
النَّاسَ، فَشَرِبُوا مِنْهَا وَسَقَوْا وزَرَعُوا ، وأصَاب طَائفَةً مِنْهَا أُخْرى إنَّما هِي قِيعانٌ ،
لا تمْسِكُ مَاءً ، وتُنْبِتُ كَلأ ، فَذلكَ مثَلُ مَنْ فَقُهَ في دِينِ اللهِ ، وَنَفَعَهُ ما بَعَثَني
الله بِهِ فَعلِمَ وَعلَّمَ، وَمَثَلُ مَنْ لَمْ يَرْفَعْ بِذلكَ رأساً ، وَلَمْ يَقْبَلْ هُدَى اللهِ الَّذي
أُرْسِلْتُ بِهِ » متفقٌ عليه

*"The guidance and knowledge with which Allah has sent me
are like abundant rain which fell on a land. A fertile part of it
absorbed the water and brought forth profuse herbage and
pasture; and solid ground patches which retained the water by
which Allah has benefited people, who drank from it, irrigated
their crops and sowed their seeds; and another sandy plane
which could neither retain the water nor produce herbage.
Such is the similitude of the person who becomes well-versed in
the religion of Allah and receives benefit from the Message
entrusted to me by Allah, so he himself has learned and taught
it to others; such is also the similitude of the person who has
stubbornly and ignorantly rejected Allah's Guidance with
which I have been sent."* [Agreed upon by Al-Bukhari and
Muslim]

[EXPLANATION OF HADITH 1379]

This is an amazing and wonderful parable mentioned here by the Prophet ﷺ and it is that the likeness of what Allah has sent of *Ilm* and Guidance is the rain. And what is meant by this, is that Allah sends the rain which gives life to the dead land, and similarly Allah's Revelation gives life to the hearts of men. Allah ﷻ likens that which He sent Prophet Muhammad ﷺ with as divine inspiration; Allah says in the *Quran*:

$$وَكَذَٰلِكَ أَوْحَيْنَآ إِلَيْكَ رُوحًا مِّنْ أَمْرِنَا مَا كُنتَ تَدْرِى مَا ٱلْكِتَٰبُ$$

$$وَلَا ٱلْإِيمَٰنُ وَلَٰكِن جَعَلْنَٰهُ نُورًا نَّهْدِى بِهِۦ مَن نَّشَآءُ مِنْ عِبَادِنَا$$

$$وَإِنَّكَ لَتَهْدِىٓ إِلَىٰ صِرَٰطٍ مُّسْتَقِيمٍ ۞ صِرَٰطِ ٱللَّهِ ٱلَّذِى لَهُۥ مَا فِى$$

$$ٱلسَّمَٰوَٰتِ وَمَا فِى ٱلْأَرْضِ أَلَآ إِلَى ٱللَّهِ تَصِيرُ ٱلْأُمُورُ$$

"And thus We have sent to you (O Muhammad) *Ruhan* (an Inspiration and a mercy) of Our Command. You knew not what is the Book, nor what is faith? But We have made it (this *Quran*) a light wherein We guide whosoever of are Slaves We will. And verily, you (O Muhammad) are indeed guiding (mankind) to the Straight Path (i.e. Allah's Religion of Islamic Monotheism). The Path of Allah, to whom belongs all that is in the heavens and all that is in the earth. Verily, all the matters at the end go to Allah (for decision). (Ash-Shura, 52-53)

The inspiration is given the similitude of rain that Allah sends down to the earth and by it, the earth becomes one of three types:

1. The earth which rain descends on and gathers for man to drink from, and it also produces vegetation and plants and so man benefits from it.
2. The earth which does not penetrate the earth but does collect for people to drink from, irrigate crops or plant vegetation.
3. The earth that devours rain but does not produce anything nor can it be used for irrigation, due it being marshy, swampy.

These are example of those who knew and taught the *Deen* and those who never raised their heads to this knowledge. The first two descriptions are of those who accepted the truth, learnt and taught others and were a benefit to themselves as well as to others. However, those who accept the truth are of two types:

1. Those that Allah has given an understanding of the *Deen*. They are able to derive rulings from the Quran and Sunnah of the Prophet ﷺ but do not teach it.
2. A mere narrator, who relates *Hadith* and memorises them but has no understanding of the *Deen*, and there are many people like this, they are mere vessels that people take from.

On the other hand those who retain this water (*Ilm*) and benefit the people with it are the people of knowledge.

So from these two just described, one safeguards and protects the *Deen*, learns and understands it and is able to produce many legal rulings from the law, their likening is that of the rain that produces great benefit to both man and produce.

And the other individual as we said mere reporter, nothing more! So they narrate but rarely memorise, their liking is to that of the earth that retains the water, and the people benefit from this in their irrigating, people still are able to benefit from persons narrations and draw rulings from them and benefit the masses with these rulings.

Back to the third type which is the earth that neither produces nor rain brings benefit nor retains water, so such land produces no benefit. So this is the liking of one which inspiration or Revelation brings no benefit to, not even the least and as we said they left not even their heads! And Allah's refuge is sought.

They forge their narrations and turn away from Allah's Commands - and we Allah ask for pardon! So look to which earth you are like, type one, which produces great benefit to vegetation, or type two or three which we seek refuge from!

In the *Hadith*, we see the outstanding teaching skills of the Prophet ﷺ whereby he used a brilliant parable and illustration to explain his intent and meaning, so as to make his words more understandable and comprehendible, as Allah ﷻ says:

مَّثَلُ ٱلَّذِينَ يُنفِقُونَ أَمْوَٰلَهُمْ فِى سَبِيلِ ٱللَّهِ كَمَثَلِ حَبَّةٍ

"The likeness of those who spend their wealth in the Way of Allah is as the likeness of a grain (of corn)." (Al-Baqarah, 261)

So, this is an example of a something similar, i.e. those who spend in Allah's cause, there are likened to the grain which grows into seven hundred grains. So whoever comprehends such parables, none will be given understanding like him. So as we said, only those who have been given *Ilm* (knowledge) will grasp such similitudes as Allah says in the *Quran*:

وَتِلْكَ ٱلْأَمْثَٰلُ نَضْرِبُهَا لِلنَّاسِ ۖ وَمَا يَعْقِلُهَآ إِلَّا ٱلْعَٰلِمُونَ

"And these similitudes We put forward for mankind, but none will grasp their meaning except those who have knowledge (of Allah and His Signs)." (Al-Ankaboot, 43)

So, such similitudes are put forth about knowledge so as to help one obtain a broader understanding of the intent; what seems worth mentioning here, O dear reader, is if you are conversing with someone, let's say an lay-man and for some reason he does not understand what you are trying to tell him, give him an example or an illustration of what you are trying to say to him as this is a very good way of making people understand what you intending by your words.

[Hadith 1380]

Sahl ibn Sa'd 🙵 reported the Prophet ﷺ said to Ali 🙵:

وعَنْ سَهْلِ بن سعدٍ ﵁ أنَّ النبي ﷺ قَالَ لِعَلِيٍّ ﵁: « فو اللَّهِ لأَنْ يَهْدِيَ اللَّه بِكَ رجُلاً واحِداً خَيْرٌ لكَ من حُمْرِ النَّعم » متفقٌ عليهِ.

"By Allah, if a person is guided by Allah through you, it will be better for you than a whole lot of red camels." [Agreed upon by Al-Bukhari and Muslim

[Hadith 1381]

Abdullah ibn Amr ibn Al-'Aas 🙵 reported the Prophet ﷺ said:

وعن عبدِ اللَّهِ بن عمرو بن العاص ﵄ أنَّ النبي ﷺ قال: «بلِّغُوا عَنِّي ولَوْ آيةً، وحَدِّثُوا عنْ بني إسْرَائيل وَلا حَرجَ، ومنْ كَذَب عليَّ مُتَعمِّداً فَلْيَتبَوَّأْ مَقْعَدهُ من النَّار » رواه البخاري.

"Convey from me even an Ayah of the Quran; relate traditions from Bani Israel, and who deliberately forges a lie against me let him have his abode in the Hell." [Reported by Al-Bukhari]

[EXPLANATION OF HADITH 1380]

The Prophet 鬱 said to Ali ibn Abi Taalib 鬱 when he gave him the flag on the Day of Khaibar:

> *"Advance with ease and gentleness until you arrive in their midst, then call to Islam and inform them of their duties to Allah in Islam. By Allah, if a person is guided by Allah through you, it will be better for you than a whole lot of red camels."*

So, the Prophet made an oath or swore by Allah, that if one man is guided by you it would better for you than red camels. So regarding red camels, then they were the favored possessions to the Arabs at that time.

So, this *Hadith* is a great exhortation and incitement in giving *Dawah* (calling people to Islam or calling them back to the truth), as well as learning and how to call to Allah the Exalted, because it is impossible to invite people Allah except by way of knowledge!

So, if one learns about Islam then calls to what he knows, this *Hadith* is proof indicating the lofty great virtue of knowledge.

[EXPLANATION OF HADITH 1381]

As for the *Hadith* of Abdullah ibn Amr ibn Al-Aas who said the Prophet 鬱 said:

> *"Convey from me even an Ayah of the Quran."*

What the Prophet ﷺ meant here is, convey and relay what I say and do to the people, meaning "What I have informed you about the Book of Allah (the Quran)," even if what you relate about (the Quran) is brief, by this what we mean here is, one should not say to people "Before I give *Dawah* (propagate or spoke) about Islam I will not do it till I first become a great Scholar!" No! Rather one may convey knowledge even if it be an *Ayah* (Verse) or short *Hadith*, but with the condition that he is certain this is an established sound statement of the Prophet ﷺ. So for this reason, the Prophet ﷺ states at the end of this *Hadith*:

> *"Who deliberately forges a lie against me let him have his abode in the Hell."*

This means, if one intentionally lies about the Prophet ﷺ, let him take his abode in the Hell-Fire, and the word used here:

فَلْيَتَبَوَّأْ

"Let him have..."

This word in this Hadith is normally used as an imperative, meaning it is an order, or *al-laamu lil amr,* the letter laam (ل) indicating a command or order. As we said it is normally used to indicate a command but here it is not used except as a predicate or *al-khabr,* meaning, certainly! So, what we are trying to say is, that it is like saying: *"Who deliberately forges a lie against me, (certainly) let him have his abode in the Hell."*

And we seek refuge from this! So in summary the intent again here is, such a person who lies against me, he is entitled to be one of the inhabitants of the Hell-Fire.

And that is because, lying about the Prophet ﷺ is not just lying upon him alone, no, rather it is also lying about Allah ﷻ, also it is lying about the *Deen*, because whatever the Prophet ﷺ was inspired with was Revelation, which is the *Deen*.

So we say, the lie told about a Scholar is not the same as a lie told about the lay-man; for example if you say regarding a particular Scholar "So-and-so says such-and-such about such-and-such matter, that this is *Haraam,* this a *Halaal,* this a *Waajib* this is Sunnah," but you are lying then this is also a very dangerous thing, due to this lie being related to things regarding the *Deen* and being related to a Scholar which as we said, the lie against the people of knowledge is greater and more severer than the lie against the lay-man.

Why do we say this? It is because the *Ulama* (Scholars), may Allah have mercy upon them, are the inheritors of the Prophets, who convey and spread the *Deen*, so evil speech regarding them is greater in sin.

With regret there are many things are circulated in public related to an Islamic awaking and that which is related to putting fear into the souls, be it through books, tapes, etc. And some of these things are nothing but pure lies about the Prophet ﷺ, so these so-called dazzling ignorant speakers spread such lies, thinking such things are important.

Even some of them know that such things are pure lies but, they insist on propagating such things. We say to them: how you can circulate such misinformation and lies fully knowing they are just that!?

We have to warn against material like this that is posted on many Masjid walls and also propagated and spoken about in the *Masaajid*, for this is where the threat comes into it which the Prophet ﷺ made, and that is: lying about him, especially when it's on purpose. As for the statement of the Prophet ﷺ:

> *"Relate traditions from Bani Israael."*

What is meant by Bani Israeel is the Jews and Christians, for if one of them says a tradition, there is no problem in relating this but with the condition that what they say does not go against the *Deen,* because some of their sayings or quotes are clear lies, and they twist and distort many things, but in saying that, it is ok to relay what we know to be a lie as to make such lies known or to expose their falsehood, and I hope the matter is clear, and Allah knows best.

[Hadith 1382]

Abu Hurayrah ﷺ reported the Messenger of Allah ﷺ said:

وعنْ أبي هُريرةَ ﵁ أنَّ رسُولَ اللهِ ﷺ قالَ : ومَنْ سلَكَ طَريقاً يَلْتَمِسُ فِيهِ عِلْماً ،

سهَّلَ اللهُ لَهُ بِهِ طَريقاً إلى الجنّةِ » رواهُ مسلمٌ

"Allah makes the way to Jannah (Paradise) easy for him who treads the path in search of knowledge."

[Hadith 1383]

He also reported the Messenger of Allah ﷺ said:

وَعَنهُ أيضاً: أنَّ رَسُولَ اللهِ ﷺ قالَ : « مَنْ دعا إلى هُدىً كانَ لهُ مِنَ الأجْرِ مِثلُ

أُجورِ مِنْ تَبِعهُ لا ينْقُصُ ذلكَ من أُجُورِهِم شَيْئاً » رواهُ مسلمٌ

"He who calls other to follow the Right Guidance will have the reward of those who follow him, without their reward being diminished in any respect on that account."

[Hadith 1384]

He also reported the Messenger of Allah ﷺ said:

وعنْهُ قال: قَالَ رسُولُ اللهِ ﷺ: «إذا ماتَ ابْنُ آدَم انْقَطَع عَملُهُ إلاَّ مِنْ ثَلاثٍ:

صَدقةٍ جاريةٍ أوْ عِلمٍ يُنْتَفَعُ بِهِ أو وَلدٍ صالِحٍ يدْعُو لَهُ» رواهُ مسلمٌ.

"When I man dies, his deeds come to an end except for three things: Sadaqatul Jaariyah (ceaseless charity); a knowledge which is beneficial, or a virtuous descendant who prays for him (for the deceased)." [All three *Hadiths* were reported by Muslim]

[EXPLANATION OF HADITHS 1382]

These three narrations clarify and show the great virtue of *Ilm*, so the first thing we would like to touch upon is the word "treads" used is the first *Hadith*: This includes one physically going out in pursuit of *Ilm*, say from one's house to a place of knowledge, be it the *Masjid*, school, college or faculty wherever that place may be. And also that which can be counted as treading a path in pursuit of seeking knowledge is one traveling from one's own country to another country to seek knowledge.

And it is narrated that Jaabir ibn Abdullah Al-Ansaari ﷺ, one of the Companions of Prophet Muhammad ﷺ, traveled the journey of one complete month on his camel in search of a *Hadith* which was narrated by Abdullah ibn Anees ﷺ from the Prophet ﷺ!

The second meaning of *"treads the path"* is the abstract meaning, which means that one acquires knowledge by way of listening to lectures of the *Ulama* or by taking knowledge from the core of the books of knowledge.

So, one who researches an issue to know a ruling pertaining to an issue in the *Deen*, even if such a person is sitting on his chair (say in his house), this is to considered treading the path seeking knowledge. And if a person sits with a Shaykh and learns from him, this is deemed treading a path in pursuit of knowledge even if he was sitting obtaining such knowledge.

So, in summary, treading the path in pursuit of knowledge in divided into two categories, first being actually going out in search of *Ilm*, second is anything that helps or aids you in acquiring *Ilm*. So, whoever treads a path in search of *Ilm,* Allah will make his way easy to *Jannah.*

Why? Because one learns about what Allah revealed as Revelation and what the Law is, and by learning and getting to know these two things one will come to know the commandments, what Allah has obligated upon mankind, also what He has forbidden them, and also what is pleasing to Allah; all these things aid as well as help one to enter *Jannah.* So know, every moment one increases and strives in obtaining knowledge, the higher his chances are in entering *Jannah.*

So, this *Hadith* is a great encouragement to seek knowledge and is clear and not hidden from any one. So, may Allah have mercy upon you, seize ever possible opportunity in seeking it, especially in your youth, which is a good time in one's life to seek *Ilm,* because what he learns will remain with him and be easier due to his youth, to memorize.

So safeguard your time and consider it precious, and immerse yourself in knowledge before a time comes upon you that will occupy you fully, you will find no time for seeking knowledge.

[EXPLANATION OF HADITHS 1383]

As for the *Hadith* of Abu Hurayrah ﷺ that the Messenger of Allah ﷺ said:

> *"He who calls others to follow the Right Guidance will have the reward of those who follow him."*

It means, on the Day of Judgment; as for his ﷺ statement:

"He who calls others to follow the Right Guidance…"

This means, he who teaches the people; so the one who calls (the people) to right guidance mentioned here in this *Hadith*, this is a person who clarifies to the people the truth and shows them the right path, he will obtain the same reward they get for guiding them to it.

Let me give an example: if a person encourages someone to pray *Witr*, like saying to them "pray make it the last prayer of the night" as the Prophet ﷺ said regarding this:
"Make your last prayer at night be Witr."

If it is because of you who urged or encouraged this person to do this, and he prayed Witr based of your encouragement, for this you will get the reward he is getting or equal to him, and also if this person urges another person to do the same, you to, will get this reward similar, till Judgment Day.

So this is proof of the great reward the Prophet ﷺ will obtain from the immense amount of people he guided and who in turn guided many, so he ﷺ will receive the reward for all these people being guided.

And with great regret, many people make the mistake of doing deeds and then saying "O Allah give the reward to Prophet Muhammad ﷺ for this deed!" And we will give an example of this, a person would perform two *Rak'at,* then say to Allah "the reward You were going to give me for these two *Rak'at,* give them to Prophet Muhammad (ﷺ)!" or a person reads the *Quran* and then says "O Allah give the reward You would of given me to Prophet Muhammad!"

This is something wrong and a big mistake that people are doing. And this habit started about three hundred years after Prophet Muhammad's 鏐 death, and some Scholars have allowed it - they say the same way you can do this for your mother and father, then you can do this with the Prophet 鏐 too.

This is a great mistake, very foolish and is a great misguidance to carry out in the *Deen*. How? We say: do you have greater love for the Prophet 鏐 than Abu Bakr? Umar? Uthmaan? Ali? Ibn Abbaas? Ibn Mas'ood or the Companions in general? The answer is certainly not, no! Did any of them ever do this: ask Allah to give the Prophet 鏐 their rewards for their good deeds? Did any of the followers of the Companions do this or any of the four great *Imams*? So if none of them ever did this, what gives you right to do it!?

All it is, is a great misguidance in the *Deen,* because as we said, all that you do of righteous good deeds, the Prophet 鏐 also gets a share in your deeds without your reward being decreased, because he first guided the Muslims to do so, therefore he gets rewarded for whatever any Muslim does whether the Muslim says "this is for you O Prophet" or not because of the Prophet's 鏐 statement:

"He who calls other to follow the Right Guidance will have the reward of those who follow him, without their reward being diminished in any respect on that account."

So we can see from this the virtue of *Ilm*, and that propagating and spreading *Ilm* is better than giving charity by far, and I will give an example of what I am trying to say: in the time of Abu Hurayrah, the kings owned the earth and in the time of

Imam Ahmed the rich gave great enormous amounts of charity away, and also in the time of Ibn Taymiyyah and Ibn Qayyim, the rich gave away plentiful charity, but the question is, where is all the fruits of so much of this charity that was given? Gone! Not a trace of it can be seen today! But on the other hand the narrations of Abu Hurayrah are constantly mentioned day and night, so he will receive the reward for all of this and also the great Imams, the same thing for them and Ibn Taymiyyah and Ibn Qayyim and other than them - they too will receive great rewards even though they are in their graves, for at the same time they are in their graves, they are teaching the Muslims their *Deen* (through their legacy of teachings) so this is proof that *Ilm* is much virtuous and better than giving charity by far.

[EXPLANATION OF HADITH 1384]

Abu Hurayrah ﷺ reported that the Messenger of Allah ﷺ said:
   "When I man dies, his deeds come to an end except for three things: Sadaqatul Jaariyah (ceaseless charity); a knowledge which is beneficial, or a virtuous descendant who prays for him (for the deceased)."

This *Hadith* encourages one to embark upon a way of using all one's time and efforts and spending all his time as well as safe guarding it to do as much righteous deeds, because he knows not when death will come upon him, (or) all of a sudden. So, he uses his time in the best way before his deeds cease and can come to an end, as these righteous good deeds will certainly

61

help him obtain a higher position with Allah the Exalted and He will greatly reward such an individual.

One is not certain when death will approach as it is not known, and as it is always unexpected and unannounced; no one is certain when death will overtake them as Allah the Exalted says:

وَمَا تَدْرِى نَفْسٌ بِأَيِّ أَرْضٍ تَمُوتُ

"And no person knows in what land he will die." (Luqmaan, 34)

If this is the case, which it is, then it is upon every person to take full advantage of his time in doing acts of obedience to Allah before such a moment overtakes him, because every soul is in a state of traversing to the abode of requital and this world is the abode of action.

The things what benefit one greatly in this life such that he reaps the fruit for them in the next are: *Sadaqatul Jaariyah* (ceaseless charity), and the things one gives in charity or building *Maasajid,* which enables people to pray, read *Quran* and teach the *Deen* and so on, and also from the things related to *Sadaqatul Jaariyah* (ceaseless charity), is things like properties, gardens and its likes which are left for the poor and needy to help them and helping students of knowledge and the *Mujaahidoon* (those who fight in the way of Allah).

Also, authoring beneficial Islamic books that aid the Muslims who will read them and benefit, whether the author of such books authored them in our time or authored them in the past. And also from the things related to *Sadaqatul Jaariyah* (ceaseless charity), are things like mending the roads and path-ways so as to prevent harm coming to the people as this is also *Sadaqatul Jaariyah*, and the origin of it is, all righteous deeds that continue after one's death are continuous and are considered *Sadaqatul Jaariyah*.

The second thing is knowledge which is beneficial, and this includes both beneficial knowledge as well as general knowledge that is useful due to the fact that the Muslims benefit greatly from this *Ilm*.

And this could be by an author encouraging his student to publish after his death books he has written while alive or a recorded lecture, so be it either while alive he encourages both or after his death, books he authored or the lectures he recorded are published for the benefit of the Muslims.

As for a virtuous descendant who prays for him (for the deceased), this includes males and females, meaning either boy or girl, and this also includes your kids or your kids' kids and so on. So one's offspring makes *Dua* for them after their death.

If on the other hand actions such as *Salaat*, reading *Quran* or giving charity were beneficial for the descendants to perform on behalf of their parents, it would be impossible for the Prophet ﷺ not to mention that they are beneficial, because as we know all that which is good and beneficial to the slave, the Prophet ﷺ guided towards and taught, whatever that thing might be.

So, why didn't the Prophet ﷺ say "Or descendants that perform *Salaat* or read *Quran* or give charity on his behalf or fasts..." since all acts of worship are righteous? But instead the Prophet ﷺ said virtuous descendants who make *Dua* (supplication). This is a proof that *Dua* is much better than these aforementioned righteous actions, otherwise the Prophet

ﷺ would have guided His *Ummah* (nation) towards doing them.

So, if was said, "which is better, giving *Sadaqah* on behalf of my dead father or making *Dua* (supplication) for him?" We say, *Dua*! As we said the Prophet ﷺ guided the *Ummah* towards that, saying:

"*Or a virtuous descendant who prays for him (for the deceased).*"

So, it is very strange that many laymen think for some reason, that *Sadaqa*, fasting and reading *Quran* for their deceased fathers benefit them (more than *Dua*)! They for some strange reason think doing these things is better than what the Prophet ﷺ said to do which was *Dua*! This is share ignorance! Those who know the text know *Dua* is far better.

Imam Maalik was asked a specific ruling which was: "Did any of Prophet Muhammad's Companions ﷺ give Sadaqah on behalf of their deceased parents?" So he replied:

"*Yes! This is no problem, but he never encouraged anyone to do this nor prompted them to do this after that.*"

Sa'eed ibn Abaadah asked a similar specific ruling to the Prophet ﷺ and asked if he could give in *Sadaqah* a garden on behalf of his mother to which the Prophet ﷺ said "yes."

Also a man came to the Prophet ﷺ and said: "My mother has died suddenly, should I give Sadaqah on her behalf? The Prophet ﷺ replied: "Yes." However these cases were specific whereas the *Hadith*: "*Or a virtuous descendant who prays for him (for the deceased),*" is general, which means it was what he legislated generally for all the *Ummah* to do, so we ask Allah to forgive us our parents and all the Muslims in general.

[Hadith 1389]

Abud'Darda reported the Messenger of Allah ﷺ said:

عَنْ أَبِي الدَّرْدَاءِ ﵁ قَالَ : سَمِعْتُ رَسُولَ اللهِ ﷺ يَقُولُ: « مَنْ سلك طَرِيقاً يَبْتَغِي فِيهِ عِلْماً
سَهَّلَ اللهُ لَهُ طَرِيقاً إِلى الجنةِ ، وَإِنَّ الملائِكَةَ لَتَضَعُ أَجْنِحَتَهَا لِطالب الْعِلْمِ رِضاً بِما يَصْنَعُ ، وَإِنَّ
الْعالِمَ لَيَسْتَغْفِرُ لَهُ مَنْ فِي السَّمَواتِ ومَنْ فِي الأَرْضِ حَتَّى الحِيتانُ فِي الماءِ ، وفَضْلُ الْعَالِمِ على
الْعابِدِ كَفَضْلِ الْقَمر عَلى سائِر الْكَواكِب، وإِنَّ الْعُلَماءَ وَرَثَةُ الأَنْبِياءِ وإِنَّ الأَنْبِياءَ لَمْ يُوَرِّثُوا دِيناراً
وَلا دِرْهَماً وإِنَّما وَرَّثُوا الْعِلْمَ ، فَمَنْ أَخَذَهُ أَخَذَ بِحَظٍّ وَافِرٍ ». رواهُ أَبو داود والترمذيُّ

*"He who follows a path in quest of knowledge, Allah will make
the path of Jannah easy for him. The Angels lower their wings
over the seeker of knowledge, being pleased with what he is
doing. The inhabitants of the heavens and the earth and even
the fish in the depth of the ocean seek forgiveness for him. The
superiority of the learned man over the devout worshipper is like
that of the full moon to the rest of the stars (i.e. in brightness).
The learned are the heirs of the Prophets who bequeath neither
dinar or dirham but only that of knowledge; and he who
acquires it, has in fact acquired an abundant good."* [Reported
by Abu Dawud and At-Tirmidhi]

[EXPLANATION OF HADITH 1389][20]

This *Hadith* also shows the virtue and great of *Ilm*! So the Prophet ﷺ says:

> *"The Angels lower their wings over the seeker of knowledge, being pleased with what he is doing. The inhabitants of the heavens and the earth and even the fish in the depth of the ocean seek forgiveness for him."*

So dear reader, be not amazed and astonished at the fact that animals ask Allah the Exalted for forgiveness for His creation! Because Allah the Exalted relates from the words of Prophet Musa:

$$قَالَ رَبُّنَا ٱلَّذِىٓ أَعْطَىٰ كُلَّ شَىْءٍ خَلْقَهُۥ ثُمَّ هَدَىٰ$$

"(Musa) said: 'Our Lord is He Who gave to each thing its form and nature, then guided it it aright.'"
(Taha, 50)

So, the animals and insects know their Lord; Allah says regarding this:

$$تُسَبِّحُ لَهُ ٱلسَّمَـٰوَٰتُ ٱلسَّبْعُ وَٱلْأَرْضُ وَمَن فِيهِنَّ وَإِن مِّن شَىْءٍ إِلَّا يُسَبِّحُ بِحَمْدِهِۦ وَلَـٰكِن لَّا تَفْقَهُونَ تَسْبِيحَهُمْ$$

"The seven heavens and the earth and all there, glorify Him and there is not a thing but glorifies His praise. But you understand not their glorifacation."
(Al-Israa', 44)

---

[20] Note: the Shaykh did not explain *Hadiths* 1385-1388.

Everything exalts and glorifies Allah and even the stones at the time of the Prophet Muhammad ﷺ used to glorify Allah and the Prophet ﷺ would hear them doing so, as Allah the Exalted is the Lord of all living creature. Allah said to the heavens and earth:

$$ اَئْتِيَا طَوْعًا أَوْ كَرْهًا قَالَتَآ أَتَيْنَا طَآئِعِينَ $$

"'Come both of you willingly or unwillingly.' They said: 'We come willingly.'" (Al-Fussilat, 11)

Allah addressed them and they responded back to Him; He said to them "come both of you willingly or unwillingly" and they responded we come willingly; so every living creature obeys Allah and is under His Command except the disbelievers from men and *Jinn*.

Allah Exalted says in the Quran many of mankind prostrate to Him and many (men) on whom the punishment is justified, He says:

$$ أَلَمْ تَرَ أَنَّ ٱللَّهَ يَسْجُدُ لَهُۥ مَن فِى ٱلسَّمَـٰوَٰتِ وَمَن فِى ٱلْأَرْضِ $$

$$ وَٱلشَّمْسُ وَٱلْقَمَرُ وَٱلنُّجُومُ وَٱلْجِبَالُ وَٱلشَّجَرُ وَٱلدَّوَآبُّ وَكَثِيرٌ مِّنَ $$

$$ ٱلنَّاسِ ۖ وَكَثِيرٌ حَقَّ عَلَيْهِ ٱلْعَذَابُ $$

"See you not that to Allah prostrates whoever is in the heavens and whoever is on earth, and the sun, and the moon, and the stars, and the mountains, and the trees, and animals, and many (men) on whom the punishment is justified." (Al-Hajj, 18)

So the disbeliever submits, not as an act of worship and nor does he prostrate to Allah as He commands them to but all have to submit to whatever Allah decrees for them in matters pertaining to what Allah legislates in His creation. This is because whatever is decreed for disbeliever, be it good or bad, they can never avoid or have any choice in such matters or flee away from matters decreed for them. Allah says:

وَلِلَّهِ يَسْجُدُ مَن فِى ٱلسَّمَٰوَٰتِ وَٱلْأَرْضِ طَوْعًا وَكَرْهًا

"And unto Allah (Alone) falls in prostrate whoever is in the heavens and the earth." (Ar-Ra'd, 15)

This form of prostration is preordained submissiveness which is a form of being under something's authority or control or governance, because no one can overcome Allah the Exalted or flee or escape from Him, as one poet from the pre-Islamic period said in his poem:

"Where will you flee to, if Allah is after you; Surely he is the loser who thinks he will flee (or escape) from Allah."

So all submit to what Allah decrees for them with or without choice; meaning, that whatever He destines for them then they cannot flee from that decree, but many on whom the punishment is justified are not those who prostrate to Him.

What more can there be than knowing the virtue of the seeker of knowledge than to know that the Angels lower their wings pleased at the actions of the seeking of knowledge! So this shows the great virtue of seeking knowledge.

In this *Hadith* of Abud'Darda, he reported that Messenger ﷺ said:

"The learned are the heirs of the Prophets."

We ask who are these heirs mentioned here in this *Hadith*? Are they those worshippers who worship Allah day and night? No! They are not! Are they the Prophets, be it whatever Prophet it may be, or his descendants? No! Rather these heirs are the *Ulama* (Scholars), as they inherit *Ilm* from the Prophets, their actions as well as their method in calling to Allah ﷻ and their guidance, proofs and evidences indicating Allah's Law (Sharia).

We see that none of the Prophet Muhammad's ﷺ descendants inherited from him, not his daughter Faatimah, his uncle Abbaas or any of his other relatives, because as we said the Prophets do not inherit Dirham or Dinaar, and this shows Allah's great wisdom; why? Because it cuts all possibilities of anyone making the claim that the Prophets' aims and purpose was purely worldly gains such as wealth and power; to prevent such false claims and to cut off all avenues, Allah did not allow them to inherit, this is why. As for the statement of Prophet Zakariyah in the Quran:

$$\text{فَهَبْ لِي مِن لَّدُنكَ وَلِيًّا • يَرِثُنِي وَيَرِثُ مِنْ ءَالِ يَعْقُوبَ}$$

"So give me from Yourself a heir, who shall inherit me, and inherit (also) the posterity of Jacoob." (Maryam, 5-6)

What is intended here is inheritance of religious knowledge and Prophethood and not wealth, because the *Hadith* states they do not inherit Dirham or Dinaar, which is a greater inheritance, so he who obtains such inheritance has obtained something abundantly great indeed. We ask Allah to make us obtain this great abundant inheritance, which is *Ilm*.

So is it not a proven fact that say, one would go as far as the east and west in search of wealth that his father left him as inheritance? Yes, one would go as far as this. If this is the case, then why would one not go this far in search of religious knowledge?

So dear reader, strive in seeking *Ilm* to your upmost, as one has to be as sincere to Allah ﷻ as he can in seeking this *Ilm*, and this is by making his leader Muhammad ﷺ in order that he worships Allah based on clear understanding. When he is making *Wudu*, he should imagine the Messenger ﷺ is in front of him making *Wudu*, so he follows and imitates him completely. And he should do likewise in the prayer and in all other acts of worship; if this was just one of the virtues of seeking *Ilm* it would be enough.

Remember *Ilm* is more virtuous than gold and silver, offspring, wives, castles and luxurious cars or anything from this world that one can amass, so we ask Allah to grant us beneficial *Ilm* and righteous actions and plentiful wealth freeing us from the need of asking His creation; indeed You (Allah) have the ability to do all things...

[Hadith 1390]

Ibn Mas'ood ﷺ reported: I heard the Messenger of Allah ﷺ saying:

عنِ ابن مسعُودٍ ﷺ قال: سمِعْتُ رسول اللَّه ﷺ يَقُولُ: «نَضَّرَ اللَّه امْرءاً سمِع مِنا
شَيْئاً ، فَبَلَّغَهُ كما سَمَعَهُ فَرُبَّ مُبَلَّغٍ أَوْعى مِنْ سَامِعٍ». رواهُ الترمذِيُّ وقال:
حديثٌ حَسنٌ صَحيحٌ

*"May Allah brighten the affairs of a person who hears
something from us and communicates it to others exactly as he
heard it (i.e., both in meaning and the words). Many a
recipient of knowledge understands it better than the one who
has heard it from."* [Reported by At-Tirmidhi who said it
was Hasan Sahih]

[Hadith 1391]

Abu Hurayrah ﷺ reported the Messenger of Allah ﷺ said:

عن أبي هُريرةَ ﷺ قال: قال رسُولُ اللَّه ﷺ: «منْ سُئِل عنْ عِلمٍ فكَتَمَهُ ، أُلجِم
يَومَ القِيامةِ بِلجامٍ مِنْ نارٍ ». رواهُ أبو داود والترمذي ، وقال: حديثٌ حسنٌ

*"He who is asked about knowledge (of religion) and conceals
it, will be bridled with a bridle of fire on the Day of
Resurrection."* [Reported by Abu Dawud and At-Tirmidhi
who said it was a Hasan Hadith]

[EXPLANATION OF HADITH 1390]

In the first *Hadith*, Ibn Mas'ood ﷺ said that the Messenger of Allah said:

> *"May Allah brighten the affairs of a person..."*

The meaning of "brighten the affairs" here means to improve, make better and radiant his affairs as Allah the Exalted says in the Quran:

$$\text{وُجُوهٌ يَوْمَئِذٍ نَّاضِرَةٌ ۞ إِلَىٰ رَبِّهَا نَاظِرَةٌ}$$

"Some faces that Day shall *Nadirah* (shining and radiant), looking at their Lord (Allah)." (Al-Qiyaamah, 22-23)

The meaning of "shining and radiant" is: good features and radiance. And when Allah says: "Looking at their Lord (Allah)," it means, looking or staring with their eyes at Allah the Exalted, may Allah make us from them! And also in the statement of the Blessed and Exalted He says:

$$\text{فَوَقَىٰهُمُ ٱللَّهُ شَرَّ ذَٰلِكَ ٱلْيَوْمِ وَلَقَّىٰهُمْ نَضْرَةً وَسُرُورًا}$$

"So Allah saved them from the evil of that Day, and gave them *Nadirah* (a light of beauty) of joy." (Al-Insaan, 11)

I.e. good features, beauty and joy - beauty in their faces and joy in their hearts.

So the Prophet's ﷺ saying: *"May Allah brighten the affairs of a person who hears something from us,"* means, he hears from us a narration or a statement, and as for the Prophet's statement: *"And communicates it to others exactly as he heard it."* What the Prophet ﷺ intended here is a form of *Dua* (supplication) for such a person who hears his *Hadith,* then informs the people about it or proclaims it as he actually heard it. So whoever delivers a narration this way, Allah will make their faces radiant of the Day of Resurrection. As for the Prophet's ﷺ statement:

"Many a recipient of knowledge understands it better than the one who has heard it."

Then this means, maybe the one who hears this narration understands it better than the one who is conveying it, and the reason is because the recipient could be more knowledgeable, understands, comprehends and grasps its true meaning and how it is applied, he applies it by putting it into practice more than the one who heard it, as the Prophet ﷺ said.

And what is acknowledged is that there are *Ulama* (Scholars) who narrate narrations, memorize them, convey them, but lack their true meaning! They convey such narrations to other *Ulama,* who on the other hand understand their intent, true meaning and how to derive and deduct many rulings from them, so this will be of great benefit to the people.

It is like we said, there is rain that falls from the sky on the land but is of no avail, neither producing benefit or producing cultivation and crops, and the opposite goes for land that this rain is of some benefit to and produces harvest; that is the similitude of the *Ulama* who understand and know these narrations and there intent, and are able to derive and deduct many rulings from such narrations.

[EXPLANATION OF HADITH 1391]

As for the *Hadith* of Abu Hurayrah, then it conveys a severe threat to those who withhold *Ilm* from those who are asked about it and are in need of such knowledge; (the threat of) bridling them with the fire on the Day of Resurrection means they will be bridled with fire on their mouths with fire, and we ask Allah for pardon!

Why such a punishment? Because one is withholding that which Allah has revealed from His Revelation which was sent with the purpose to be propagated to guide the people.

So if you know that someone is seeking guidance and information it is impermissible for you to withhold such knowledge if you are fully aware of such knowledge. But as for if someone came to you merely testing you then you are not obliged to answer him, you have a choice whether to answer or not; Allah says regarding this in the Quran:

فَإِن جَآءُوكَ فَٱحْكُم بَيْنَهُمْ أَوْ أَعْرِضْ عَنْهُمْ وَإِن تُعْرِضْ عَنْهُمْ

"So if they come to you (O Muhammad), either judge between them, or turn away from them. Turn away from them." (Al-Maa'idah, 42)

Here, Allah knew that these people merely came just asking or to know whether the Prophet ﷺ knew the answer and not for a purpose other than this. So in summary, if you fear answering someone's question will lead at that time to a greater *Fitnah* (trail), then again in this case you are allowed to put off such a reply till a later date, this is ok so as to avoid greater *Fitnah*, and Allah grants success.

[Hadith 1392]

Abu Hurayrah ☺ reported that the Messenger of Allah ﷺ said:

وعنه قال: قال رسولُ اللهِ ﷺ: « مِنْ تَعَلَّمَ عِلْماً بِما يُبْتَغَى بِهِ وَجْهُ اللهِ عز وَجَلَّ لا يَتَعَلَّمُهُ إلا لِيصِيبَ بِهِ عرضاً مِنَ الدُّنْيا لَمْ يَجِدْ عَرْفَ الجِنَّةِ يوْم القِيامةِ » يعني: ريحها، رواه أبو داود بإسناد صحيح.

"He who acquires knowledge with the sole intention of seeking the Pleasure of Allah but for worldly gain, will not smell the fragrance of Jannah on the Day of Resurrection." Meaning: Its scent. [Reported by Abu Dawud with an authentic Isnad]

[EXPLANATION OF HADITH 1392]

Ilm (knowledge) is between two categories:
1. Knowledge which is sought for the pleasure of Allah such as knowledge of the fundamentals of Islam as well as knowledge of the Arabic language.
2. Knowledge of worldly matters such as engineering, mechanics, construction and the like.

Before mentioning the first category, I will briefly mention the second category which as we know, there is no problem in working to provide for one's family. And also there is no problem in learning engineering to become an engineer so one can obtain with such profession a job and the same with mechanics also. So seeking knowledge or learning such trades or such professions with the intention of acquiring a means of sustenance for oneself is okay. But in saying this it would be better for a Muslim to make his intention when studying these subjects pertaining to worldly matters to benefit the Muslims with such skills such as engineering, mechanics, construction and the like; then this will be of great virtue for him and the reason is, so that he intends two things: a worldly benefit plus a reward for his intent to serve the Muslims and benefit them.

So for example, if he intends to learn such trades so as to avert the Muslims as a whole from utilising the services of the *Kufaar*, then this is a very good intention no doubt. And again, say on the other hand he just makes his intention to learn, such as mechanics or to allow him to obtain lawful provisions, then again this is okay, because business and trade are lawful as a means to increase one's wealth.

Now regarding the first category, then it is regarding learning the religious fundamental of Islam regarding Allah ﷻ. Such *Ilm* should only be sought with the sole purpose of seeking Allah's pleasure and His reward.

If such knowledge is sought seeking worldly gains and for other than Allah's pleasure and reward, such a person will be prevented from smell the fragrance of *Jannah* of the Day of Resurrection. This is why the threat is so severe regarding this, and it indicates seeking *Ilm* in the *Deen* for other than Allah's sake is counted as one of the major sins, and such actions are devoid of benefit.

For example, someone says "I will seek *Ilm* so as to make peoples' heads turn towards me, so that they show respect and honour me more," or a person says "I am only seeking this *Ilm* (of the *Deen*) so that it will be a means of provisions for me," and the like: such individuals, and we seek refuge with Allah, will not smell the fragrance of *Jannah* on the Day of Judgment. And there has been some difficulty between many who seek *Ilm* in such places like colleges, schools, and Islamic centers who do so to only obtain certificates!

Another person says, "I will seek *Ilm* until I am able to be a teacher at an educational department, but with the purpose of benefitting the people with this *Ilm* or I will obtain the certificate to become a head in a distinguished Islamic department; this type of intention one makes is good and allowed and void of sin.

With great regret, in this times we are living in, it seems to be the peoples' greatest concern in obtaining graduation certificate from such universities! So, you see many people obtaining leading positions of authority on various Islamic sciences in universities, colleges, faculties and schools, and as we said, such people gain lofty positions, but they are the most ignorant of the people!

It could be the case that some students in only secondary school studying Islam are much more knowledgeable than this person who has a certificate! And this is not something I am making up or giving as an example, this is something with regret that is happening as we speak!

You even have those who have these certificates with these fancy titles: such as Doctor, who has no *Ilm* whatsoever in the least maybe because he graduated and obtained his certificate by way of deception or his *Ilm* is only on a superficial level and not that he really understands due to the fact that the *Ilm* never really stayed in his mind when he was learning, say due to forgetfulness, but you will see such individuals being given such position clearly based upon such certificates!

At times you would find a good student of knowledge, a great benefit to the people and to himself one thousand times better than this so-called certificate holder, but with regret this student of knowledge would be refused to teach *Deen* to the people merely because they say he has no certificate, or he has not studied in one of these faculties. Why!?

So, as we said with great regret, the times have greatly changed and the aim of things and pursuit of things is wealth (money). We say in summary: if the purpose of one's pursuit of *Ilm* (of the *Deen*) is to benefit oneself and the people and not solely for worldly gains then as we said, this is okay and such a person does not fall under the threat this *Hadith* contains.

And all praise is to Allah; indeed actions are by intentions, and one will get what he intended, and this is the distinguishing factor, so look to what your heart is intending!

So it is upon the seekers of knowledge in these universities, if it is solely for the purpose of obtaining only certificates or just so you can be like so-and-so who has such-and-such position with such-and-such income, we say to such people: is this what you want? If they say "yes, this is what I want!" We say to them: this is harmful and obnoxious and you will become a loser if this is your intention! But if he says "the only way these places such as *Masaajid*, schools, centers etc., accept anyone who wants to teach is if they have such certificates, and I want to benefit the people with this *Ilm*, so this is the reason why I am striving to obtain such certificate so as to be in the service to those who are in need of such knowledge, and I am not striving for position and worldly gain, so this is my aim as well as purpose," then we say: this is a very good intention you have, and this something noble and no sin is on you for what you have intended. As indeed actions are by intentions, and one will get what he intended.

O student of knowledge! Be aware of having the wrong intention! Because the knowledge of this *Deen* is lofty, great and honorable, and should not be sought as a means to wealth and fame! This world with its wealth and what it offers, what is it? Food, drink! What happens next, where does this food and drink end up? In no other place except as waste flushed down the toilet!

So, one has to remember either he will leave this world or this world will leave him. Where does wealth end up? When you die where does it go? Its goes. All what you obtained and acquired from it goes to, as is known, someone else.

But on the other hand, regarding the affairs of the next life like righteous good deeds such as seeking *Ilm*, why would you do an injustice to yourself by using the *Ilm* of Allah's great Religion, by way of these lowly worldly non-valuable things, to seek purely worldly gains at the expense of Allah's great pleasure? Surely this is an indication of one's shortsightedness and is clear misguidance.

We have to remember to make this *Ilm* for Allah's sake, to protect Allah's Law and as a means to raise ignorance from oneself as well as others such as fellow Muslims, and do not forget this *Ilm* is inheritance from the Prophets, as we stated earlier.

So we ask Allah to make us more sincere to Him and rectify our actions. Indeed He has the ability to do all things!

[Hadith 1393]

Abdullah ibn Amr ibn Al-Aas ﷺ reported: I heard the Messenger of Allah ﷺ say:

وعنْ عبدِ الله بن عمرو بن العاص ﷺ قال : سمِعتُ رسولَ اللهِ ﷺ يقول: «إنَّ اللهَ لا يقْبِض العِلْمَ انْتِزَاعاً ينْتزِعُهُ مِنَ النَّاسِ، ولكِنْ يقْبِضُ العِلْمَ بِقَبْضِ العُلَماءِ حتَّى إذا لمْ يُبْقِ عالماً ، اتَّخَذَ النَّاسُ رُؤوساً جُهَّالاً فَسئِلُوا ، فأفْتَوْا بِغَيْرِ علمٍ ، فَضَلُّوا وأَضَلُّوا» متفقٌ عليه.

"Verily, Allah does not take away knowledge by snatching it from the people, but He takes it away by taking away (the lives of) the religious Scholars till none of them remains. Then the people will take ignorant ones as their leaders, who when asked to deliver religious verdicts, will issue them without knowledge, the result being that they will go astray and will lead others astray." [Agreed upon by Al-Bukhari and Muslim]

[EXPLANATION OF HADITH 1393]

We see from this *Hadith* that *Ilm* will be taken away, and to the point that not a Scholar will be left to guide the people to Allah's *Deen*, then the *Ummah* will go astray, and the Quran will be taken away, from the *Muslims* hearts and the *Masaahif* (written copies) and the people of the *Sunnah* have said:

> "*Indeed the Quran is the revealed Speech of Allah, other than created, and it will (in the last before Judgment Day) be taken away.*"

And the meaning of "*will be taken away*" is that it (the Quran) will be raised back up to Allah the Exalted in the last days. And this will be a time when the people will abandon the Quran totally. They will not read it and they will neither live by it nor practice it!

So as we said the passing away of the *Ulama* will happen then, not one Scholar will be left; then people will take their ignorant ones as their leaders (as their *Ulama*), so these ignorant so called leaders will give rulings without *Ilm*. By this they will lead astray and are astray themselves, and we seek refuge from this! So Islam will be left to the likes of these ignorant ones, and it will fade away until what was known to be Islam in its pure form, and what we mean by this is what is built upon from the Quran and the Sunnah, will become something unrecognisable and this is inevitable.

This is all by the passing away of the *Ulama*, so this *Hadith* is an encouragement in seeking *Ilm*, and to be cautious and warn and show the importance of seeking *Ilm*; it does not indicate that one should merely be aware of the matter and submit, no, rather it is an incitement to seek *Ilm* and safeguard this matter and for us all to be on our guard if such a time comes upon us.

So as we said, the fact that the Prophet ﷺ informed us of such a time coming upon us does not mean that he intended by it an acceptance for what is to occur, no, rather it is similar to his statement:

"You will follow those who came before you."

And what the Prophet ﷺ meant in this *Hadith* is, that you will embark upon their way, those who came before you, so the Companions ﷺ said to him, "Do you mean the Jews and Christians?" He ﷺ replied:

"Yes the Jews and the Christians."

So, the Prophet ﷺ informing us that the Muslims will follow them is as a means to warn and make us aware of the matter so as to be cautious and not that we should follow them; it is a mere enlightenment of the matter so as to also make us aware as to what will happen to the Muslims if they do not follow his guidance.

In short, it is upon us to know the difference between when the Prophet ﷺ was informing us about something to occur and when he was warning us about a matter to safeguard us from it.

This *Hadith* is informing us that the *Ulama* will die and the ignorant will be left and at the head of those involved in delivering religious verdicts will lead astray as well as being astray themselves, so we ask Allah the Exalted to grant us beneficial *Ilm*, righteous acceptable deeds and abundant provisions!

باب التقوى

THE CHAPTER ON RIGHTEOUSNESS

TRANSLATOR'S PREFACE

All praise and thanks be to Allah the Supreme and the Exalted, the only One deserving to be worshipped, and peace and blessing be showered upon His noble Messenger and may peace and blessing be bestowed upon his Companions, those whom Allah chose to carry a heavy responsibility for us, and peace also be upon those who follow in their footsteps till the Day of Resurrection.

I selected the chapter of *Taqwah* (translated as righteousness) because I find this one of the hardest of matters, and one of the matters I would love to learn more about in order to increase my own level of *Taqwah* and strive for Allah's sake to be counted among those who surely do fear Him as well as wanting the same for you, all my brothers and sisters.

It seems that *Taqwah* is a matter no Muslim can say they have enough of. But awareness and understanding everything pertaining to *Taqwah,* its linguistic meaning, its technical definition, the Quranic verses regarding it and the many *Ahaadith* encouraging it will surely help fulfil their thirst for an increase in their level of *Taqwah Inshaa'Allah.*

Regarding *Taqwah,* Allah the Exalted and High says in the Quran:

وَلَقَدْ وَصَّيْنَا ٱلَّذِينَ أُوتُواْ ٱلْكِتَٰبَ مِن قَبْلِكُمْ وَإِيَّاكُمْ أَنِ ٱتَّقُواْ ٱللَّهَ

"We have recommended to the people of the Scriptures before you that you (all) fear[21] Allah and keep your duty to Him." (An-Nisaa'a 131)

Al-Baghawi comments about this verse:

"This Verse means that it is upon an individual to take none alongside Allah in worship, and be completely obedient to Him."[22]

From this statement of Imam Al-Baghawi, we infer that one should be as obedient as he or she is able to, as obedience to Allah is an act of fearing Him. So what seems to be apparent from this verse is that it is a command from Allah the Exalted to fear Him, just as He has commanded every Muslim to pray, fast, obey one's parents, avoid *Zinaa* or whatever unlawful matter there is – in the same manner, He the Exalted commands that He be feared. This indicates that one has to fear Allah as much as he or she is able. Listen to the great Imam of Yemen, Ash-Shawkaani, and what he said about this verse.

"In this verse, Allah is commanding the believer to fear Him."[23]

---

[21] Ibn Munthir said: The word Fear in the language means to frighten. (*Lisaanul Arab* 2/1292, see also *Tafsirul Qurtubi*) The legal definition of fear is defined as: fearing Allah the Exalted. Abu Qaasim said in this respect: "Whoever fears something runs away from it and whoever fears Allah runs to Him." (*Ihya Uloom* 4/153)

[22] *Tafsirul Baghawi* 2/297.

So, the understanding of this Verse is, it is *Waajib* (obligatory) to fear Allah, and if one does not then one may be counted as being sinful. At-Tabari also said:

> *"This means, be very cautious of that which you are doing and stay away from disobeying Allah and going against His orders and commands."* [24]

Al-Qaasimi also said about this verse:

> *"This is advice from Allah Himself that those before as well as us should fear Him, single Him out in worship alone and avoid making partners in worship with Him."* [25]

Shaykh Muhammad Abdi and Shaykh Muhammad Rasheed Ridaa said:

> *"This verse means, one should uphold the Sunnah, and stick to Islam and implement the Law."* [26]

As-Suyuti and Al-Mahalli also said:

> *"What Allah means is: one should fear His punishment and this is done by obeying Him."* [27]

And, dear readers, may Allah have mercy upon you, what are the things that lead one to Paradise? Surely one of the greatest things and at the top of the list is *Taqwah*. Abu Hurairah

---

[23] *Fathul Qadeer* 1/682.

[24] *Jaami'-ul Bayaan* with Shaykh Mahmood Shaakir's *Ta'leeq* 5/370.

[25] *Tafsirul Qaasimi* 3/365.

[26] *Tafsirul Manaar* 5/381.

[27] *Tafsirul Jalaalayn* p221 in English by Daarut Taqwah

reported that the Messenger of Allah ﷺ was asked about which thing will enter a man into Paradise. He replied:
"Fear of Allah and good manners." [28]

Ibn Al-Arabi mentions the following about this *Hadith*:
"One must fear Allah while he is alone or while he is among any group of people, whether they are pious or impious. The person must tend to himself and cannot use an excuse for disobeying Allah." [29]

Al-Mubaarakfoori said about *Taqwah*:
"Taqwah is the foundation on the religion." [30]

And Ibnul Mutazz said in a line of poetry regarding *Taqwah*:
"Abandon grave and minor sins, for this is the essence of fearing Allah. Do as a man walking in a road full of thorns who avoids what he sees. Do not make little of a minor sin. A mountain is made from pebbles." [31]
Ibn Juzayy Al-Kalbi said:

---

[28] *Sunan At-Tirmidi* (2004), *Al-Adabul Mufrad* (289), *Sunan Ibn Maajah* (4246), *Musnad Ahmed* and others. Shaykh Al-Albaani ﷺ said this *Hadith* is *Hasan* in his checking of *At-Tirmidi* and this *Hadith* is a longer *Hadith* but we have summarised it for the purpose of what we need it for, whoever wants to refer to this *Hadith* in full length refer to any of the above references.

[29] *Aaridhat Al-Ahwadhi bi Sharh Sahih At-Tirimidi* 8/154-155.

[30] *Tuhfah* 6/122.

[31] *Jaami'ul Uloom wal Hikam*, page 402.

"The key that help to attaining Taqwah revolves around ten matters. If a person takes these matters seriously the result should be a true Taqwah in his heart:

1. *Fear of punishment in the Hereafter.*
2. *Fear of punishment in this world.*
3. *Hope of reward in this world.*
4. *Hope of reward in this Hereafter.*
5. *Fearing the reckoning and accountably of one's deeds.*
6. *Feeling shameful that Allah should see oneself performing deeds that are displeasing to Him.*
7. *Being thankful and feeling grateful for all of the bounties that Allah has bestowed on that person.*
8. *The true knowledge or reality of Allah, His Names and attributes, as Allah says:*

   "Those who truly fear Allah among His servants are only the people of knowledge." (Al-Faatir 28)

9. *Having a great deal of respect for the greatness of Allah.*
10. *Being sincere and truthful in one's love for Allah.*[32]

I sincerely ask Allah to accept this from me and make it be of great benefit to the dear reader. Indeed Allah has the ability to do all things.

---

[32] Ibn Juzayy Al-Kalbi v1 p36

Allah the Exalted says:

يَـٰٓأَيُّهَا ٱلَّذِينَ ءَامَنُوا۟ ٱتَّقُوا۟ ٱللَّهَ حَقَّ تُقَاتِهِۦ

"O you who believe! Fear Allah as He should be feared."
(Aali Imraan 102)

Also Allah says:

فَٱتَّقُوا۟ ٱللَّهَ مَا ٱسْتَطَعْتُمْ

"So, keep your duty to Allah and fear Him as much as
you can." (At-Taghaabun 16)

This second Verse explains the meaning of the first one. Allah also
says:

يَـٰٓأَيُّهَا ٱلَّذِينَ ءَامَنُوا۟ ٱتَّقُوا۟ ٱللَّهَ وَقُولُوا۟ قَوْلًا سَدِيدًا

"O you who believe! Keep your duty to Allah and fear
Him, and speak (always) the truth." (Al-Ahzaab 70)

Allah the Exalted and High says:

وَمَن يَتَّقِ ٱللَّهَ يَجْعَل لَّهُۥ مَخْرَجًا ۞ وَيَرْزُقْهُ مِنْ حَيْثُ لَا يَحْتَسِبُ

"And whosoever fears Allah and keeps his duty to Him,
He will make a way for him to get out (from every
difficulty). And He will provide him from (sources) he
could never imagine." (At-Talaaq 2-3)

He also says:

إِن تَتَّقُوا۟ ٱللَّهَ يَجْعَل لَّكُمْ فُرْقَانًا وَيُكَفِّرْ عَنكُمْ سَيِّئَاتِكُمْ وَيَغْفِرْ لَكُمْ ۗ وَٱللَّهُ
ذُو ٱلْفَضْلِ ٱلْعَظِيمِ

"If you obey and fear Allah, He will grant you *Furqaan* (a criterion to judge between right and wrong), and will expiate for you your sins, and forgive you; and Allah is the Owner of great bounty." (Al-Anfaal 29)

[THE DEFINITION OF TAQWAH]

The word "*Taqwah*" (التَّقْوَى) is a noun derived from the root word "*Wiqaayah*" (الوِقَايَة) which means, "To protect."

When it refers to Allah it means, "to protect oneself from Allah's (anger and) punishment." So, one protects himself from Allah's punishment by performing what Allah has commanded and refraining from what He has prohibited. And know that at times the word *Taqwah* comes alongside the word *Birr:* (البِر) which means obedience, righteousness, virtue. So, regarding this word *Taqwah* Allah the Exalted says in the Quran:

$$وَتَعَاوَنُوا۟ عَلَى ٱلْبِرِّ وَٱلتَّقْوَىٰ$$

"Help one another in *Birr* and in *Taqwah* (piety)." (Al-Maa'idah 2)

So, if the word *Birr* comes with the word *Taqwah* in the same sentence, then the word *Birr* means, "Fulfilling a commandment," and as for the word *Taqwah*, it would mean, "Refraining from a sin." But if *Taqwah* is used alone or by itself, then it means as we said: performing what Allah has commanded and remaining away from what He the Exalted has prohibited.

So, the Exalted has mentioned in the Quran that Paradise is prepared from the *Muttaqoon* (the pious who fear Allah) and the people of *Taqwah* are the people of Paradise. May Allah make us and you of them! So, it is an obligation upon the people to fear Allah the Exalted by fulfilling His commandments, and to request from Him His great rewards

He has prepared for the God-fearing and ask Him to be saved from His punishments. Then the author Imam An-Nawawi ﷺ mentions the following verses related to *Taqwah*:

[EXPLANATION OF SUPPORTING VERSES]

Allah ﷺ says from the first of these verses:

يَـٰٓأَيُّهَا ٱلَّذِينَ ءَامَنُواْ ٱتَّقُواْ ٱللَّهَ حَقَّ تُقَاتِهِۦ

"O you who believe! Fear Allah as He should be feared." (Aali Imraan 102)

Allah the Exalted, directs this command to the believers, as the believers acquire *Emaan* (faith) based upon how much *Taqwah* they exert. As for His words: **"Fear Allah as He should be feared"** Then the author (Imam An-Nawawi) explains its meaning by the next verse after this one, on how Allah should be feared:

فَٱتَّقُواْ ٱللَّهَ مَا ٱسْتَطَعْتُمْ

"So, keep your duty to Allah and fear Him as much as you can." (At-Taghaabun 16)

Meaning, fear Allah to the best of your ability and as much as you can, as the Allah the Exalted burdens not a soul beyond its capability. So, it is not intended to mean help one another upon righteousness no, rather what its intent is, an incitement and encouragement to fear the Exalted to the best of one's capability. So, it's your capability and you trying your hardest to fear Him, this is what counts, as a soul is not put to task what is beyond its ability. And also what we also benefit from this verse is that if a person finds difficulty in completely fearing Allah, then you should still try to exert himself (or herself) in the best way possible to fear Allah. As the Prophet ﷺ said in a *Hadith* narrated by Imraan Ibn Hussain:

> *"Pray standing, and if you're unable, then sitting, and if you're unable then now (pray) on your side."*

So here, the Prophet ﷺ laid down what is one's duty, that is, firstly praying standing and if one finds that hard then sitting and if one finds it hard and is unable, then one lies down and prays. And this is not just restricted to this matter, rather it is for all the rest of the tenets of Islam that one finds difficult, including fasting, and that is if one cannot fast during the month of Ramadan, he may make up those days he was unable to fast, as Allah the Exalted says in the Quran:

$$وَمَن كَانَ مَرِيضًا أَوْ عَلَىٰ سَفَرٍ فَعِدَّةٌ مِّنْ أَيَّامٍ أُخَرَ$$

"And whoever is ill or on a journey, the same number of days (which one did not fast must be made up) from other days." (Al-Baqarah 185)

And on the same token regarding Hajj Allah ﷻ says:

$$وَلِلَّهِ عَلَى ٱلنَّاسِ حِجُّ ٱلْبَيْتِ مَنِ ٱسْتَطَاعَ إِلَيْهِ سَبِيلًا$$

"And *Hajj* (pilgrimage to *Makkah*) to the House (*Ka'bah*) is a duty that mankind owes to Allah, who can afford it." (Aali Imraan 97)

This shows that whosoever is unable to perform the *Hajj*, then the obligation is lifted from that individual period. But on the same note, if you have finical means to perform it, but physically you are unable, in that case one can appoint someone else to perform it on his (or her) behalf and that is also applicable to *Umrah* (minor *Hajj*).

So, in short, when fearing Allah without these restrictions and hardships, then the conclusion is that one fears Allah by keeping to His commands and refraining from His prohibitions to the best of one's ability. And to add to this point, whosoever is forced, compelled or coerced to do something Allah has forbidden him, Allah has allowed and given concession to do that forbidden act to prevent harm coming to that individual and this is found in the words of Allah when He says:

وَقَدْ فَصَّلَ لَكُم مَّا حَرَّمَ عَلَيْكُمْ إِلَّا مَا ٱضْطُرِرْتُمْ إِلَيْهِ

"He has explained to you in detain what is forbidden to you, except under compulsion of necessity." (Al-An'aam 119)

Even if a person is compelled to eat dead meat, swine, the meat of a donkey or generally any forbidden meat, it would be permissible as a means to prevent harm coming to that individual.

Regarding the next verse pertaining to *Taqwah* Allah ﷻ says:

يَـٰٓأَيُّهَا ٱلَّذِينَ ءَامَنُوا ٱتَّقُوا ٱللَّهَ وَقُولُوا قَوْلًا سَدِيدًا

"O you who believe! Keep your duty to Allah and fear Him, and speak (always) the truth." (Al-Ahzaab 70)

Here Allah commands the believers to the two following matters:
1. To fear Him.
2. To speak the truth and what is correct.

Taqwah we have previously explained, as for speaking the truth, then this means speaking that which is correct. This includes every word pertaining to good, whether that is statements of remembrance (*Thikr*), seeking *Ilm* (knowledge) or ordering good or forbidding bad, or general statements like good words which are a means that create love and harmony between the people, or words or statement similar to this, as the Prophet ﷺ said:

> *"Whoever believes in Allah and the last Day, should either speak good or remain silent."*

The opposite of this, is other than a truthful correct word, and that is a word other than that which is correct, and that could be something said pertaining to a matter or a place. As for to what is pertaining to a matter, it could be an indecent vile word, and that could be related to cursing, insulting, backbiting or tale-bearing and whatever is similar to these things.

As for something pertaining to a place then this means, this word or statement in and of itself is correct but, it is said in an unsuitable place because every statement has its prescribed time and place. So in light of this, this would be considered other than correct, even though this word in and of itself is not *Haraam* (unlawful). So, we will give you an example to clarify our point: say if an individual happened to see a person involved in a forbidden matter and he advises this person regarding this impermissible act, there are conditions related to advising someone or reprimanding them, and it could be that advising that person at that particular time is inappropriate and unsuitable. So in this case, this would be considered incorrect and inappropriate. So regarding *Taqwah*, we say, if a person fears his Lord, he acquires the two following benefits, Allah says (in the following verse):

$$ يُصْلِحْ لَكُمْ أَعْمَـٰلَكُمْ وَيَغْفِرْ لَكُمْ ذُنُوبَكُمْ $$

"He will direct you to do righteous good deeds and will forgive you your sins."

1. So, with *Taqwah*, Allah corrects affairs and directs towards good.
2. And with it, He forgives sin.

And what is worth mentioning is, one who does not fear Allah the Exalted but maybe does speak the truth or say what is correct, this person will neither be directed to good and righteous deeds nor have his affairs mended nor will he (or she) have their sins forgiven. So, what we see from this verse is an incitement and a great encouragement to fear Allah the Exalted as well as the immense virtue in doing so. Allah the Exalted says:

$$ وَمَن يَتَّقِ ٱللَّهَ يَجْعَل لَّهُ مَخْرَجًا • وَيَرْزُقْهُ مِنْ حَيْثُ لَا يَحْتَسِبُ $$

"And whosoever fears Allah and keeps his duty to Him, He will make a way for him to get out (from every difficulty). And He will provide him from (sources) he could never imagine." (At-Talaaq 2-3)

100

This means: the one who fears Allah is the one who is deemed as fulfilling Allah's orders and leaving what He forbids him, and the fruit of fearing Allah is: **"He will make a way for him to get out."** What this means is, from every hardship, adversity or misfortune one maybe experiencing; so every time a person is undergoing difficulties which pull him (or her) to the ground, the more this individual is God-fearing, Allah the Exalted will open a way to get this God-fearing person out of that situation. And this could be pertaining to matters regarding wealth, his offspring, or generally in life and the likes, whatever the matter which he (or she) maybe undergoing or facing. So have sure faith that Allah for certain will make a way out for you in your affairs, because it is only a matter of the Exalted to merely utter the statement: **"Be and it is."**

We say again! How many in reality feared Allah, the One who should only be feared, and He the Exalted made a way out of their difficult situation! Many, in fact too many, has it not reached you of the story the three who were trapped in the cave![33] A huge rock fell in front of the cave door trapping them in the cave, and they were unable to move it due to its huge size, so they all implored to Allah using their most sincere righteous deeds as a means to intercede for them to Allah to free them from this cave, which they were trapped in. Each one invoked Allah for help and to rescue them. So, Allah ﷻ opened up the way for them and Allah shifted the rock for them and they were able to walk free out of that cave. And as

---

[33] The Shaykh ﷺ mentions this amazing *Hadith*, which is a very long *Hadith*, but for some reason or the other he has only mentioned it in brief, for further reference, see Al-Bukhari 2272 and Muslim 2743.

we said, there are so many examples of similar cases. Allah the Exalted says regarding *Taqwah*: **"And He will provide him from (sources) he could never imagine."** So, this also is plain to see, another tremendous great benefit of the fruits of fearing Allah and that is that He the Exalted provides for the one who fears Him provisions from where that individual imagines not. And as is our habit to make a matter clearer we will give you another example: if an individual obtains wealth through an unlawful way or means, and we happen to know this individual, and we advise him and due to this he refrains from this sinful way of acquiring wealth, then Allah the Exalted has given His word He will certainly provide for this individual, no doubt.

But, O reader, do not be hasty! Do not think if you are not given in replacement something automatically that your giving up this *Haraam* act was in vain! No, rather Allah could be testing this individual by delaying that thing he is expecting as a means to merely test him; yes this is possible. Allah could be merely delaying rewarding him the fruit for his labour, why? He could be testing this person to see if he will simply return to that wrong action, will he or not? Another example, if you work in a bank which is involved in *Ribah* (usury), and you got advice to leave that job and you do, but after leaving that job, one month goes by and still you find no lawful work, two months go by still no work, grieve not and nor be saddened or say strange unfamiliar words; don't let even a single bad word come out of your mouth or the likes, avoid all statements similar to, "Where is such provision promised to me, from where I expect not!" Wait, patiently and have sure faith in Allah's promise, and know He never breaks His promises, so believe what He has said and surely you will be given, and be not impatient as the Prophet said in a *Hadith*:

> *"The supplication of every one of you will be granted if he does not get impatient and say (for example): I supplicated my Lord but my prayer has not been granted."*

So, be patient, avoid the *Haraam* Allah has forbidden upon you, and wait for a way then Allah will grant you from where you know not. Allah the Exalted says regarding *Taqwah*:

$$ إِن تَتَّقُواْ ٱللَّهَ يَجْعَل لَّكُمْ فُرْقَانًا وَيُكَفِّرْ عَنكُمْ سَيِّئَاتِكُمْ وَيَغْفِرْ لَكُمْ وَٱللَّهُ ذُو ٱلْفَضْلِ ٱلْعَظِيمِ $$

"If you obey and fear Allah, He will grant you *Furqaan* (a criterion to judge between right and wrong), and will expiate for you your sins, and forgive you; and Allah is the Owner of great bounty." (Al-Anfaal 29)

In this verse are the following three enormous benifits:

1. **"He will grant you *Furqaan*"**

    This means He will give a criterion to be able to judge between what is right and what is wrong and between what is harmful and what is beneficial. Included in this category is *Ilm* (knowledge), and what we mean is, that Allah the Exalted bestows upon an individual an understanding of the *Deen* (Religion) and a vast comprehension of it that none has been bestowed unto like him. As certainly *Taqwah* is a means to attaining increased *Al-Huda* (guidance), *Al-Ilm* (knowledge) and his *Al-Hifz* (memorization), and it is worth

The Chapter on Righteousness

mentioning what has been related from Imam Ash-
Shaafi'i when he said:

> *"I complained to Waki' about my poor
> memory; so he advised me to abandon sins and
> he said: "Know that knowledge is light, and
> the light of Allah is not bestowed upon the
> sinner."*

So, there is no doubt, the more a person increase in
knowledge, naturally he increase in learning and
differentiating the truth from falsehood. Furthermore,
Allah allows the servant to reach a level whereby He
bestows upon him a good understanding. Why? This is
because *Taqwah,* is surely a means for strengthening
one's understanding, and strong understanding assists
in increasing *Ilm.* For example, you see two men
memorizing a verse from the Book of Allah; one of
them can extract from it three rulings, whilst the other
is able to extract more than this, according to that
which Allah has blessed upon him from the
understanding of the *Deen.*

So, *Taqwah* is a means for increasing *Ilm* as well as
insight; Allah has blessed the one who has *Taqwah*
with insight with which he is able to distinguish even
among the people. So, from simply seeing a person, he
is able to know whether he is honest or dishonest or
pious or obscene, such that it is possible that he is able
to judge a person whom he has not met and does not
know anything about him because of what Allah has
given and blessed him with in terms of strong insight.

From the many virtues the God-fearing are bestowed with are miracles that none other than them are honored with. And from these miracles is what happened to many of the Companions and their followers; from them is what happened to Umar Ibn Khattaab. One day he was delivering the Friday sermon on Friday in the *Masjid* in *Al-Madinah,* so to the amazement of the Companions they heard him say during the midst of his sermon: *"O Saariyah the mountain! O Saariyah the mountain!"*

So, the people were amazed at how someone during the sermon would say something like this, and the reason why he was saying this was because Allah the Exalted showed him the Muslim army whose leader and commander in Iraq whose name was Saariyah Ibn Zaneem; the enemies had cornered them so Allah the Exalted exposed their location to Umar as if he was actually witnessing or seeing them with his own eyes. So he called on Saariyah to seek shelter in the mountain. Saariyah heard Umar calling out to him even though Umar at the time was in *Al-Madinah.* So, all of this was solely because of (Umar's) *Taqwah,* as these types of miracles that have happened to the God-fearing are nothing but rewards from Allah to these individuals due to the depth of fear these individuals have for Him the Exalted and High.

2. "And will expiate for you your sins"

Expiation of evil deeds is done by good actions, as good actions expiate evil deeds as the Prophet ﷺ said in a *Hadith*:

> *"The five prayers and from Jumah prayers to the next Jumah prayer, and from fasting one Ramadan to fasting the next Ramadan is an expiation for that which occurs between them, so long as the major sins are avoided."*

Also the Prophet ﷺ said:

> *"The performance of an Umrah to the performance of the next Umrah is expiation for that which occurs between them."*

3. "And forgive you"

This means Allah ﷻ made it easy upon His slaves to turn to Him in seeking forgiveness and *Tawbah* and certainly this is a great blessing bestowed upon His slaves. From the afflictions that have befallen many is, the undermining and disregarding their sins! So because of this the person persists upon these sins considering them minor and not even giving thought to them, and we seek refuge from this! Allah says regarding this in the Quran.

قُلْ هَلْ نُنَبِّئُكُم بِالْأَخْسَرِينَ أَعْمَـٰلاً • ٱلَّذِينَ ضَلَّ سَعْيُهُمْ فِى ٱلْحَيَوٰةِ ٱلدُّنْيَا وَهُمْ يَحْسَبُونَ أَنَّهُمْ يُحْسِنُونَ صُنْعًا

"Say (O Muhammad): Shall We tell you the greatest losers in respect of (their) deeds? Those whose efforts have been wasted in this life while they thought that they were acquiring good by their deeds." (Al-Kahf 103-104)

So, with regret, many are unable to distance themselves from sins and their plough has become one of sheer pity and despair and we seek refuge in Allah! The more they increase in sin the harder it gets to abstain and give up those sins; to add to that, the more these sins seem to be trivialized the more they are considered ok; and as is known, some sins are considered so deadly they can blind a person completely to the point that such a person no longer knows the difference between right and wrong. But, it is not so for those who are God-fearing.

As we know if an individual is in the constant habit of fearing Allah, Allah Himself helps this individual, by preventing him from sinning and He makes it easy for this person to refrain from doing that sin until Allah forgives him, and it is possible that Allah forgives this person merely because of this person's *Taqwah*. This is what happened to the Companions who took part in battle of *Badr*, and for this reason the Prophet ﷺ said:

"Allah has already looked at the Badr warriors and said: 'Do whatever you like, for I have forgiven you.'"

So, what they fell into from sin Allah forgave them, and that was due to what they endured from the many hardships that befell them such as the many battles they fought and encountered so many difficulties therein.

"And Allah is the Owner of great bounty." This means, He the Exalted, if He says this is how He is, that is confirmation that He is bountiful and bestows plenty. One of the reasons here why He states in this verse He is the Owner of great bounty is it will strongly increase a person's urge to want to seek the many abundant bounties He possesses, is this not right? So know, *Taqwah* as we said, means fearing Him; it is defined also as fleeing and turning back to Allah the Exalted and Allah knows best.

[Hadith 69]

Abu Hurairah ﷺ reported: It was asked:

يا رسولَ اللَّهِ مَن أَكْرَمُ النَّاسِ ؟ قال : « أَتْقَاهُمْ » فَقَالُوا : لَيْسَ عَنْ هَذا نَسْأَلُكَ،
قَالَ : « فَيُوسُفُ نَبِيُّ اللَّهِ ابن نَبِيِّ اللَّهِ ابن نَبِيِّ اللَّهِ ابن خَلِيلِ اللَّهِ » . قَالُوا : لَيْسَ
عن هَذَا نَسْأَلُكَ ، قال : فَعَنْ مَعَادِنِ الْعَرَب تسأَلُوني؟ خِيَارُهُمْ في الْجَاهِلِيَّةِ
خِيَارُهُمْ في الإسلام إذَا فَقُهُوا » متفقٌ عليه.

"O Messenger of Allah! Who is most honourable amongst mankind?" He ﷺ said: *"The most pious of them."* They said: "We are not asking about this." He ﷺ said: *"Then the most honourable of men was Yusuf (Joseph), the Prophet of Allah, who was the son of Khaleel of Allah (i.e., Ibraheem)."* They said: *"We are not asking you about this."* He enquired: *"Are you then asking about the classes of Arabs? The best of them in the Pre-Islamic Period of Ignorance are the best of them in Islaam, provided they comprehend the religious knowledge."* [Agreed upon by Al-Bukhari and Muslim]

[EXPLANATION OF HADITH 69]

Regarding the statement: "O Messenger of Allah! Who is most honourable amongst mankind?" The Prophet ﷺ said: "*The most pious of them.*" This means whoever is the most honourable among the people he is the one who is considered the most pious of people. So the Prophet's ﷺ answer coincides identically with the statement of Allah when He says in the *Quran*:

$$إِنَّ أَكْرَمَكُمْ عِندَ ٱللَّهِ أَتْقَنَكُمْ$$

"Verily the most honourable of you in sight of Allah is that (believer) who has *Taqwah.* " (Al-Hujuraat 13)

This shows that Allah the Exalted does not look at one's genealogy or lineage or social status such as wealth or beauty; rather, He looks at one's action. Knowing this, it only aids and greatly encourages those who are God-fearing, and this is because Allah confirms they are the best of the people to Him: those that manifested to Him piety outwardly as well as inwardly. So, this *Hadith* is a great incitement and an encouragement towards fearing Allah the Exalted, as those who fear Him are given this noble title and that is they are the most honourable in His sight. So, the Companions never intended this question when they asked the Prophet ﷺ, rather they said: "We are not asking about this." Then the Prophet ﷺ mentioned to them that Yusuf was the most honourable of mankind, who was the son of one of Allah's Prophets and He is Yusuf the son of Yaqoob son of Ishaaq son of Ibraheem. So he was a Prophet from the descendants of many Prophets of

Allah, and for this reason he was considered the most honoured of mankind. So, they (the Companions) then said: "We are not asking you about this." He enquired: *"Are you then asking about the classes of Arabs?"* So this word: *"Classes of Arabs"* refers to their origin and their lineage.

As for the Prophet's ﷺ words: *"The best of them in the Pre-Islamic Period of Ignorance are the best of them in Islam, provided they comprehend the religious knowledge."* This means, the most honourable of people pertaining to genealogy, origin, and class are those who had the best lineage, origin, and class before converting to Islam; however this has a condition, and the condition is that they comprehend the *Deen*. So for example, Banu Haashim (the descendants of Haashim) they were the most notable well known Arabs of Quraish (of Makkah), so if they enter into Islam they would be considered the best people. But, as we said, only if they learn and comprehend the religion. And the opposite is said, and that is if they do not learn and comprehend the *Deen* even though they were from the dignified tribe or leaders, then they are not seen as the best and most honourable of people in the sight of Allah.

This hadith is a proof for the following: people are given virtue by their lineage but as we have said that is if they have an understanding of the *Deen*. So, there is no doubt that some tribes or lineages do have some virtue over others and for this reason Banu Haashim was of the most virtuous Arab tribes and this was the Prophet's ﷺ tribe and he was the most noblest of creation as Allah says in the *Quran*:

$$ٱللَّهُ أَعۡلَمُ حَيۡثُ يَجۡعَلُ رِسَالَتَهُۥ$$

"Allah knows best where to place His Message." (Al-An'aam 124)

So, if this tribe was not deemed the most notable of tribes the Prophet (Muhammad) ﷺ would not have originated from them, so this is an indication of this tribe's superiority among the other many tribes, and so the proof of the lofty status of this tribe is in the words of the Prophet ﷺ in this *Hadith* when he said: *"The most pious of them."* Surely the more obedient you are to Allah and fear Him then the more you counted the most honorable in His (Allah's) sight, and we ask Allah to make us from those who truly fear Him ﷻ.

[Hadith 70]

Abu Sa-id Al-Khudri reported the Prophet ﷺ said:

« إنَّ الدُّنْيا حُلْوَةٌ خَضِرَةٌ ، وإنَّ اللَّهَ مُسْتَخْلِفُكُمْ فِيهَا . فيَنْظُرُ كَيْفَ تَعْمَلُونَ . فَاتَّقُوا الدُّنْيَا واتَّقُوا النِّسَاءِ. فَإِنَّ أَوَّلَ فِتْنةِ بَنِي إِسْرائيلَ كَانَتْ في النساء » رواه مسلم.

"The life of the world is sweet and green. Allah makes you generations succeeding one another so that He may try you in respect to your actions. So beware of the allurement (trails) of this world and those of women. The first trail of the Banu Isra'eel was through women." [Reported by Muslim]

[EXPLANATION OF HADITH 70]

The author (Imam An-Nawawi) mentions this *Hadith* and that is because of the command of the Prophet ﷺ after mentioning the life of this world, that a person should fear Allah; the Prophet ﷺ said: *"The life of the world is sweet and green"* - sweet means, it is considered beautiful and attractive to a person, and the reason why the life of this world is described as sweet and green is because these two things normally are pleasant to people or highly considered in peoples view. So one's eyes normally pursue what it likes firstly, then his (or hers) desires after that. So we say, if an individual yearns as well as craves for these two as we have just described, it is feared that person will strongly indulge in them. So, this world deludes and deceives the people and makes them yearn, long, as well as crave to devour it more and more. Its deceptiveness is so great that this life makes you have no desire for anything other than it and nothing is sought after with the in-depth burning desire and yearning similar to it or equal to it.

But the Prophet ﷺ explained that Allah ﷻ has placed us in the earth to see how we act and behave, what will we put forward; at the top of the list in our lives is submission to Allah and obedience to Him; will we be of those who, while on this earth, resist and restrain their desires and put first that which Allah has commanded and that is to obey Him as well as being aware not to be deceived by this passing short worthless degrading life or on the other hand will it be the opposite of what we have said?

As for the Prophet's ﷺ statement: *"So beware of allurement (trails) of this of this world"* What does this mean? It means fulfilling and implementing that which you have been commanded to, and staying away from that which you have been commanded to avoild and to not be easily deceieved by this world and its dazzling amazements and beauties as Allah says in thr Quran:

$$\text{إِنَّ وَعْدَ اللَّهِ حَقٌّ فَلَا تَغُرَّنَّكُمُ الْحَيَوٰةُ الدُّنْيَا وَلَا يَغُرَّنَّكُم}$$

$$\text{بِاللَّهِ الْغَرُورُ}$$

"Verily the promise of Allah is true, let not then this (worldly) present life deceive you, nor let the chief deceiver (Satan) deceive you about Allah." (Luqmaan 33)

The Prophet ﷺ then said: *"So beware of the allurement (trails) of this world and those of women."* This means, be aware, very alert and cautious of women! And this includes being wary and cauious from the plain deceit from one's own wife as well as her craftiness and also being cautious of unrelated females, and for this reason the Prophet ﷺ next said in the *Hadith*: *"The first trail of the Banu Isra'eel was through women"* And this means, that they were put to trail through women, and the women were astray and they led the men astray, and we seek Allah in Allah from this! And we see our enermies and the enemies of Islam in our times, thier only focus seems to be on matters related to women and women only! The focus is on how they look, mixing with them in work places and the likes and they (the non-Muslims) seem to only live life like to that of a animal, and the only thing that matters in their lives are the private parts and the stomach, and Allah's refuge is sought! Women are viewed as toys or somewhat like dummies and nothing more than a mere object of satisfation, and all that matters is her figure, form and shape. Their main consideration is looks and beauty and this is by way of books and magazines, and in them her hair, skin, and legs are the main centre of attention.. And these womenfolk have no concern for religion nor worship and some of them have no liking for even kids.

So, our enermies and the enemies of the *Deen* of Islam as well as those who display little shame, they prompt and incourage womenfolk to wonder the market places till they incite the men in them to overly fantasize about them and this puts a strain upon these men; and as we know those who are prone to such great trails and afflications are mostly the young, those who have plenty of spare time on thiers hands and the rich. As the poet said:

"Indeed the youth, free time and the wealth,
Surely these are destructive indeed these are destructive."

So, as we said our enemies only desire is to cause curruption between the young men and women out there, and what does this do to the youth? Well, it causes free mixing between the two sexes, it incites the youth to indulge in fornication as well as other lude practises such is glancing to these female which is the fornication of the eyes and it causes unnecessary talking between both sexes which again is fornication of the tongue and touching which occurs between both genders, and this is the fornication of the hands and lastly, the actual act itself (fornication) which both may commit and all this occurs due to the woman being in the same places as men.

What then, are the other forms of corruption that occur from free-mixing of the two sexes at places of work? As is known, a woman has the recommended place, and that is her home, so if she leaves her domain or say, her husband's home to work, or in search of work, then how is it possible for this family unit to be united? Certainly it well be the opposite, and that is divided and unstable.

And surely if the women are out working most of the time then certainly the house hold will be in need of someone else to look after and take care of it, and that will cause them to be in need of a maid or servant. So, in this case these women will search across the entire earth in search of a maid, and this will mean that non-Muslims will enter her home, and we know, many of the other faiths lack manners and good conduct and this could lead to many evils occuring. So these maids are made to live at such dwellings to maintain them while these women are out making a living, they become at such work places the focus of attention and this leads the men to only be concerned with these women.

And from the other great curroptions caused by women free mixing with men, is that it leads to the break down of that family and this is due to the fact the children of that household, if they are not cared for and looked after by thier mother but by a servant, for sure these children will naturally forget thier parents and create disorder and mayhem in that home for certain.

There is no doubt the enemies which come from our own ranks of Muslims, who go to study in non-Muslim countries will and surely have been affected by the non-Muslim way of thinking, rather they have been brainwashed, and these things that they will be thinking, all contridict the faith of Islam.

And we do not say they go against our *Aqeedah* rather we say they destroy it! And why we say this is because, some of the disbelievers say Allah has a partner as well as those who say there is no God (atheist) and simillar statements. So the people will remain like animals neither bothering with *Aqeedah* nor worship; rather, thier only concern is the life of this world with its adornments and women and as this is what the Prophet ﷺ told the Muslims: *"I'm not leaving a trail more harmful for men than the Fitnah of women."*

So it becomes a must upon us and the Muslim *Ummah* (nation) regarding our enemies and their way of thinking to stand up to do the opposite and oppose such ways, thoughts and words that accrue, wherever we may be and whatever place that maybe. We have to remember and not forget that the aim of the non-Muslims is to wipe Islam out and destroy all Muslim countries, especially Makkah and Al-Madinah.

So ever country must look to see how much it is preserving it's faith and has it been affected by the corruption of the non-Muslim influences; at the same time when the Muslim countries become badly influenced, their honour fades, that is due to the plots to corrupt and destroy the Islamic countries, so much so that other Muslim countries will watch these countries struggling with these influences and say, how will this Islamic country act!? Will it behave according to how the *Deen* legislates, which is built upon preserving one's faith, *Deen* and honour, which will certainly strengthen and give honour to that country and will the Muslims prevent it from disgrace, humiliation as well as dishonour. So in short we say, it is upon us, and our brothers in faith and upon the youth, the Scholars and callers to Islam to denounce the way and thinking these people have promoted and act in opposition to it as they surely leads one to the Blazing Fire; we ask Allah the Exalted to make such plots and plans go in vain and to not give our enemies any victory and to make the righteous men among us stand firm upon this great *Deen* to repel those who desire to corrupt us through such matters which we have said are their goals; indeed Allah is All-Generous, All-Kind!

[Hadith 71]

Abdullah Ibn Mas'ood ﷺ reported that the Messenger ﷺ used to say:

«اللَّهُمَّ إِنِّي أَسْأَلُكَ الْهُدَى وَالتُّقَى. وَالْعَفَافَ وَالْغِنَى » رواه مسلم .

"*Allahumma inni as-alukal-huda wat-tuqa wal-'afaafa wal ghina (O Allah! I ask You for guidance, and piety, chastity and self-sufficiency).*" [Reported by Muslim]

[EXPLANATION OF HADITH 71]

This was the *Dua* that the Prophet ﷺ would make and invoke Allah with. So what is the meaning here of the word: *"Guidance"*? Guidance here means *Ilm* (knowledge). He is asking for Allah the Exalted for *Ilm,* so He the Prophet was like everyone else, and that was that he was in great need of *Ilm,* because Allah the Exalted said in the Quran:

$$ فَتَعَلَى ٱللَّهُ ٱلۡمَلِكُ ٱلۡحَقُّ ۗ وَلَا تَعۡجَلۡ بِٱلۡقُرۡءَانِ مِن قَبۡلِ أَن يُقۡضَىٰٓ $$

$$ إِلَيۡكَ وَحۡيُهُ ۖ وَقُل رَّبِّ زِدۡنِي عِلۡمًا $$

"And be not in haste (O Muhammad) with the Quran before its revelation is completed on you, and say: "My Lord! Increase me in knowledge." (Ta-Ha 114)

Also Allah Says:

$$ وَعَلَّمَكَ مَا لَمۡ تَكُن تَعۡلَمُ ۚ وَكَانَ فَضۡلُ ٱللَّهِ عَلَيۡكَ عَظِيمًا $$

"And taught you that which you knew not. And ever great is the Grace of Allah unto you (O Muhammad)." (An-Nisaa' 113)

So, this is an indication that the Prophet himself was in great need of *Ilm,* so this is why He would ask Allah the Exalted and High for guildance.

This word guidance, if it is mentioned by itself then it means *Ilm* and success and guidance to the truth and if it appears alongside something else then it indicates and is explained to mean *Ilm*, and the reason why it is explained as such is the *Waw Al-Attaf* means in the Arabic language: incompatible or contrary; in short it means that the word guidance has one meaning and the word after it has another meaning. So for the next word to be explained from this *Hadith*: *"O Allah! I ask You for guidance and piety,"* then ppiety has another meaning as well as any word that comes along side it.

The word *"Piety"* means fear of Allah ﷻ. So the Prophet ﷺ would ask His Lord for piety, i.e. that Allah makes him successful in obtaining piety or fear of Him. And this is because Allah the Exalted is the giver who bestows upon mankind all their needs, as man is in the state of loss, so if Allah bestows upon a person the trait of fear, then this person will surely become upright and fearing of Allah ﷻ.

As for the word after this: *"And Chastity"* What is intended here is abstinence from all that Allah the Exalted has forbidden or modesty. The letter *Waw* here after the word, "Piety," is made specific over the general; that is, it is specific in the thing being mentioned and it is synonymous. and what we mean is, when one asks for the chastity as is a specific thing, then this includes him and all those under his guardianship such as his family members, and as for supplication for chastity for others, this is said as a general supplication. So in short, abstinence means, refraining from all that the Exalted has prohibited.

As for the word: *"And self-sufficiency"* What is meant by this is, one frees himself from want and from anyone other than Allah. If Allah makes a individaul successful and makes him free from relying upon His creation, this individaul becomes within themself honourable and noble and free from debasement, for without doubt, relying upon Allah's creation dishonours the self as well as humillitates it. We have said turning to Allah the Exalted increases one's honour and is a noble act of worship and that is asking the Exalted for one's needs to be met. It is upon us to implement the Prophet's ﷺ example, and that is by using this *Dua* (supplication) in asking and requesting Allah to give us guildence, piety, chastity and self-sufficiency, and in this is proof that the Prophet ﷺ had no ability to bring good to himself nor prevent harm befalling himself.

This *Hadith* invalidates the claims of those who call upon and make *Dua* to their so-called helpers and those righteous individuals they call upon for their needs to be met as well as to prevent harm and bring benifit! And sadly this is what is done by the ignorant folk who make *Dua* to the Prophet ﷺ whenever they are at his grave side. And others call upon thier so-called supporters for help and thier needs to be met other than Allah ﷺ; these individuals are clearly astray in the religion and short-sighted, as those they are calling upon have not got the abillity to either bring harm nor prevent it themselves as Allah says to the Prophet in the Quran:

$$\text{قُل لَّآ أَقُولُ لَكُمۡ عِندِى خَزَآئِنُ ٱللَّهِ وَلَآ أَعۡلَمُ ٱلۡغَيۡبَ وَلَآ أَقُولُ لَكُمۡ إِنِّى مَلَكٌ}$$

"Say (O Muhammad): "I don't tell you that with me are the Treasures of Allah, nor (that) I know the unseen; nor I tell you that I am an Angel." (Al-An'aam 50)

Also the Exalted says:

قُل لَآ أَمْلِكُ لِنَفْسِى نَفْعًا وَلَا ضَرًّا إِلَّا مَا شَآءَ ٱللَّهُ

"Say (O Muhammad): 'I possess no power of benefit or hurt to myself except as Allah wills.'" (Al-A'raaf 188)

Also Allah says:

قُلْ إِنِّى لَآ أَمْلِكُ لَكُمْ ضَرًّا وَلَا رَشَدًا • قُلْ إِنِّى لَن يُجِيرَنِى مِنَ ٱللَّهِ أَحَدٌ وَلَنْ أَجِدَ مِن دُونِهِۦ مُلْتَحَدًا

"Say: 'It is not in my power to cause you harm, or to bring you to the Right Path.' Say (O Muhammad): 'None can protect me from Allah's Punishment (if I were to disobey Him), nor should I find refuge except in Him.'" (Al-Jinn 21-22)

So, mankind must realize that no matter what Allah bestows upon them from the likes of prestige, honour or status, this does not give them the right to be called upon in supplication! Rather, such individuals will denounce those who called upon them instead of Allah ﷻ; and as Eesa (Jesus) himself says when Allah asks Him:

وَإِذْ قَالَ ٱللَّهُ يَٰعِيسَى ٱبْنَ مَرْيَمَ ءَأَنتَ قُلْتَ لِلنَّاسِ ٱتَّخِذُونِى وَأُمِّىَ إِلَٰهَيْنِ مِن دُونِ ٱللَّهِ قَالَ سُبْحَٰنَكَ مَا يَكُونُ لِىٓ أَنْ أَقُولَ مَا لَيْسَ لِى بِحَقٍّ

"O Jesus, son of Mary! Did you say unto men: 'Worship me and my mother as two gods besides Allah?' He well say: 'Glory be to you! It is not for me to say what I had no right to say.'" (Al-Maa'idah 116)

So, this clearly shows that Eesa or anyone else, does not have the right to say to anyone to take them as a Lord and God other than Allah ﷻ. The verse continues:

إِن كُنتُ قُلۡتُهُۥ فَقَدۡ عَلِمۡتَهُۥ ۚ تَعۡلَمُ مَا فِى نَفۡسِى وَلَآ أَعۡلَمُ مَا فِى نَفۡسِكَ ۚ إِنَّكَ أَنتَ عَلَّـٰمُ ٱلۡغُيُوبِ

"'Had I said such, You would surely have known it. You know what is in my inner-self though I do not know what is in Yours, truly, You only You, are the All-Knower of all that is hidden and unseen.'" (Al-Maa'idah 116-117)

So in short, what we hear from some of these deviant Islamic groups who go to the graves claiming they assist them when their call upon them, this is surely a great deviation in the religion of Islam and shows how short-sighted these astray people are with such claims, for how can someone dead, motionless and in his grave at all be of any assistance! How can they help when these individuals have passed away many years ago and cannot even hear their *Dua* (supplication)! Certainly Allah grants success!

[Hadith 72]

Adi Ibn Haatim At-Ta'i ﷺ said: I heard the Messenger of Allah ﷺ say:

« مَنْ حَلَفَ عَلَى يَمِين ثُمَّ رَأَى أتقَى للّهِ مِنْها فَلْيَأْتِ التَّقْوَى » رواه مسلم

"He who has taken a oath (to do something) but found something else better that that (which brings him closer to Allah), then he should do that which is better in piety (and he should expiate for that breaking of oath)." [Reported by Muslim]

[EXPLANATION OF HADITH 72]

The oath mentioned here in this *Hadith* is to make an oath in Allah's Name or to swear to do something in Allah's Name from His many Names or attributes, and in saying this it is not permissable to swear by any of His Prophets, Angesl or any of His creation as the Prophet 🕌 said:

> *"Whoever makes an oath then he should make it in Allah's Name, if not he should remain silent."*

Also the Prophet 🕌:

> *"Whoever swears by other than Allah has committed disbelief and associated a partner with Allah."*

So, whoever swears by other than Allah has committed a sin and his oath he made does not count and this is because it is not in conformity with that which the Prophet 🕌 legislated as he said in a *Hadith*:

> *"He who does something contrary to our way will have it rejected."*

So know, that it is not befitting that a person makes excessive oaths all the time as Allah says regarding this in the Quran:

$$\text{وَٱحْفَظُوٓاْ أَيْمَٰنَكُمْ}$$

"And protect your oaths." (Al-Maa'idah 89)

Regarding this verse some of the Quran commentators have said: "This means do not make excessive oaths all the time but in any case if one does want to make an oath then he should restrict it to saying: "I swear by Allah if Allah so wills."

So, by expressing it in this format one obtains the two following benefits:

1. Allah makes that affair easy for that individual.

2. If one expresses ones oath using this term and changes one's mind afterwards, one will not have to make an expiation.

So, regarding making an oath for something in the future this entails expiation if one does not fulfill that oath he (or she) makes, but as for making an oath or swearing by Allah pertaining to something in the past this does not entail making expiation but if an individual does swear by Allah related to something in the past the least we say regarding this is that such a person is a sinner; if on the other hand he is telling the truth then there is no sin upon him and we will give an example to explain what we are trying to say: if an individual says: "I swear by Allah I did not do it" swearing by Allah related to something in the past, whether he lies or speaks the truth, he need not make expiation. But regarding something pertaining to the future, then in this case one has to make expiation and again we will give an example, so say an individual says: "I swear by Allah I will not do it." If one does what he has sworn or made an oath not to do, in this case he (or she) has to offer expiation, but if he does not do it then there is no expiation upon he (or her).

In any case, is it better for me to swear I will not do something or not swear at all? This *Hadith* mentions that the

Prophet ﷺ explained that if a person finds that which is better after he has made an oath to do something, then he should expiate for that oath he made then do the new thing that was considered better. So if it was said: "I swear by Allah I will not talk to him," we say, if it was a Muslim you said this about then, in this case it would better to talk to this person you have sworn not to talk to and make expiation for your oath, as swearing not to talk to a Muslim forever is forbidden in Islam. Also if an individual says: "I swear by Allah I will not visit my relatives," we say, if you say such a thing, then offer expiation for swearing that you would not visit your relatives, then after that visit them, as it is not allowed to sever ties with one's relatives, so one should do what is better as the Prophet ﷺ said:

"And consider something better than it, make expiate for your oath and choose the better alternative."

Allah grants success.

[Hadith 73]

Abu Umaamah ⬥ said: I heard Messenger of Allah ﷺ during the sermon of the Farewell Pilgrimage saying:

عنْ أبي أُمَامَةَ صُدَيَّ بنِ عَجْلانَ الْبَاهِلِيّ رضي اللَّهُ عنه قال: سَمِعْتُ رسول اللَّه
صَلَّى اللهُ عَلَيْهِ وسَلَّم يَخْطُبُ في حَجَّةِ الْوَدَاعِ فَقَالَ: « اتَّقُوا اللَّهَ ، وصَلُّوا
خَمْسكُمْ ، وصُومُوا شَهْرَكمْ ، وأَدُّوا زَكَاةَ أَمْوَالِكُمْ ، وَأَطِيعُوا أُمَرَاءَكُمْ ، تَدْخُلُوا جَنَّةَ
رَبِّكُمْ » رواه التِّرْمذِيُّ ، في آخر كتابِ الصلاةِ وقال : حديثٌ حسنٌ صحيح .

"Be mindful of your duty to Allah; perform your five daily Salaat (prayers), observe Saum (fast) during the month (of Ramadan), pay the Zakat on your properties and obey your leaders; (if you do so) you will enter the Jannah of your Lord."
[Reported by At-Tirmidhi]

[EXPLANATION OF HADITH 73]

Regarding the Prophet's ﷺ types or categories of admonishing, then they are divided into two:
1. General
2. Due to a reason.

As for first of the two, then they were the admonishments which were general such as during *Khutbahs* on Friday and admonishing (his Companions) on the day of *Eid*. But regarding the eclipse prayer, and whether he ﷺ would address or admonish his Companions, then the *Ulama* differ over this matter, one group considered it to be the first type which was the general admonishment while the other though it was the second type, which was due to a pressing need! So, the reason why they differ was due to the fact that the solar eclipse only happened once during the time of the Prophet ﷺ. So, after he had prayed the prayer of this eclipse he Prophet ﷺ stood up and admonished his Companions. So some *Ulama* say that this was considered from the first type which falls under the general type. They go on to say, what the Prophet ﷺ legislated and he himself did and continued doing, is what we act upon and this only occurred once during his life so how can we say that it was due to a reason?

As for the second group, then they say no, rather it was due to a reason! But what seems to be correct and the closer opinion to the truth is, it was from the first type (general type), as it is the *Sunnah* (a recommended act and not compulsory or required) upon the Muslims after the prayer to address and admonish the people, rather than it being an encouraged act. So, as for the second type (due to pressing need), then it is from the likes of the following and we will mention a *Hadith* to demonstrate what we mean:

The Prophet ﷺ addressed and admonished the people when Usaamah Ibn Zayd tried to intercede for a noble woman from the *Makzoomiyah* tribe when she borrowed people's belongings and did not return them. So, the Prophet ﷺ ordered that her hand be cut off. So this greatly concerned the *Quraish* of *Makkah*, so they sent Usaamah Ibn Zayd to the Prophet ﷺ to intercede with the Prophet ﷺ regarding her so that the Prophet ﷺ would not cut off her hand and to pardon her; so Usaamah pleaded with the Prophet ﷺ to which the Prophet ﷺ said to him:

> *"Do you intercede when one of the legal punishments ordained by Allah has been violated?"* Then he got up and addressed the people saying: *"The people before you were ruined because when a noble person amongst them committed theft, they would leave him, but if a weak person amongst them committed theft, they would execute the legal punishment on him."*

(So back to the first type which is the general type of admonishing), the Prophet ﷺ addressed and admonished his Companions in the farewell pilgrimage (*Hajjatul-Wadaa*) on the day of *Arafat*, and similarly, he addressed his Companions on the day of *An-Nahr*, so these admonishments fall under the first category which is a general admonishing the Prophet ﷺ gave. In the admonishing he gave in the farewell pilgrim He addressed the people as follows:

> *"O mankind be dutiful to you Lord,"*

And these words of the Prophet ﷺ correspond with the words of Allah when He says in the Quran:

يَـٰٓأَيُّهَا ٱلنَّاسُ ٱتَّقُواْ رَبَّكُمُ

"O mankind be dutiful to you Lord." (An-Nisaa' 1)

So, the Prophet ordered them all to fear Allah the Exalted and be dutiful towards Him who created them and who bestowed upon them much good from His Bounty and He allowed them to accept His Message through His Prophet ﷺ; the Prophet ﷺ next said:

"Perform your five daily Salaat (prayer)."

So, these five prayers are the same prayers that Allah the Exalted imposed upon the Prophet ﷺ.

As for the Prophet's ﷺ next statement: *"Observe Saum (fast) during the month,"* it refers to fasting in the month of Ramadan.

As for the Prophet's ﷺ statement: *"Pay the Zakaat on your properties";* this means: give those who are deserving of your *Zakaat* and be not stingy and or a miser.

As for the Prophet's ﷺ last statement in this *Hadith: "Obey your leaders";* this means, those who Allah the Exalted has placed in authority over you, and this includes the following:

1. Those in authority over your land or country (like Makkah and *Al-Madinah*).
2. Those in authority in government (like a prime minister) or state leaders.
3. Those in authority such as the president.

So, it is upon the subject to obey those in authority but this has a condition and that is: only obey them in obedience to Allah, but as for disobedience to Allah then this is unlawful and forbidden, even if that is what they command, as obedience to the Creator takes precedence over obedience to His creation as Allah says in the Quran:

يَٰٓأَيُّهَا ٱلَّذِينَ ءَامَنُوٓاْ أَطِيعُواْ ٱللَّهَ وَأَطِيعُواْ ٱلرَّسُولَ وَأُوْلِي ٱلۡأَمۡرِ مِنكُمۡ

"O you who believe! Obey Allah and obey the Messenger (Muhammad), and those of you (Muslims) who are in authority." (An-Nisaa' 59)

In short, it means that obeying the authority is *Waajib* (an obligation) after one obeys Allah and His Messenger. So know, that obedience to the Prophet ﷺ is in in fact obedience to Allah, and this is because the Prophet ﷺ never commanded anything except that Allah was pleased with that. And the reason why those in authority are mentioned lastly, after Allah and His Messenger ﷺ, is because, obedience to Allah and His Messenger ﷺ comes first then those in authority next and not the other way around. And it could be that those in authority command that which is displeasing to Allah, so this is why those in authorities are mentioned in the verse lastly.

So, one is forbidden to disobey those in authority if what they command is not counted as a sin in the *Deen* of *Islam*, and with regret some ignoramus people say the authority obligate upon us such-and-such but we do not see this in the Quran and the *Sunnah*! So (they say) in this case we are not obligated to obey those in authority over us!

We say: this is none other than sheer ignorance! Rather, they have missed the point and that is, yes, what those in authority command is in the Quran and *Sunnah*, and that is because Allah and His Messenger ﷺ have commanded plainly to obey those in authority, so those who claim otherwise are completely wrong, as Allah clearly says: **"O you who believe! Obey Allah and obey the Messenger (Muhammad), and those of you (Muslims) who are in authority."**

It is also confirmed through many *Ahaadith* that the Prophet ﷺ commanded obedience to one's ruler or those in authority and from them is this *Hadith* at hand.

As we know, obedience to Allah and to Messenger ﷺ is compulsory whether those in authority are those who command us or not, we still have to obey them, as this is obedience to Allah and His Messenger ﷺ. So we round up by saying the following, the Prophet's ﷺ last speech was what? It was those things that were most important and they were? From them was what is mentioned in this *Hadith* as well as many other matters, so it is upon the Muslims to submit to the commands that the Prophet ﷺ advised the people to cling to and Allah knows best.

باب حسن الخلق

THE CHAPTER ON GOOD MANNERS

TRANSLATOR'S PREFACE

I say to you, I am greatly in need of this book, which is one of the reasons why I focused my time on it; I am presenting to you this explanation on good manners and character, advising myself first and then you to have good manners. I say this with the intention that I will try to live by what I am preach, hoping Allah will rectify my ways, and make me a better Muslim *Inshaa Allah*! In my quest to make a change in my life, I am hoping you too can join me in trying to obtain a more refined character and lofty manners. I say, by effort, practice and constant self-reminding, we will be able to change our character and behavior as bad traits can be changed and they are not fixed or permanent, no! If that were the case, Allah would not oblige a Muslim to have good character since there would be no means to develop such character.

I will briefly mention a few sayings from the *Salaf* in a hope that you will, before reading this book, understand what our forefathers had to say about good manners, character and noble behavior, but I will first mention what the Prophet ﷺ said about one of the reasons he was sent by Allah the Exalted and High:

"I was sent to perfect good character."[34]

Al-Baaji said about this *Hadith*:

> *"The Arabs were of those who had the best of manners, and the reason for this was because what remained of the Law of Prophet Ibraheem, and as time passed this somewhat changed dramatically, so Allah the Exalted sent Prophet Muhammad ﷺ to perfect good character and to clarify where they had gone astray and what was an obligation upon them regarding Islam.* [35]

Ibn Abdil Birr also said:

> *"This is an indication that righteousness, piety and good manners are all part of the Religion, as well as virtue, a sense of honour, generosity, performance of good deeds and justice: all of these things the Prophet ﷺ was sent to perfect.*[36]

Ibn Qayyim said about good manners and character:

> *"All of the Religion is good behavior and Khuluq (character). What increases you in (good) behavior increases you in religion."*[37]

Ibn Qayyim also said:

---

[34] *Al-Adabul Mufrad* (273) and others. Shaykh Al-Albaani graded it *Sahih* in his *Silsilatuss-Sahihah* 45.

[35] *Al-Muwatta* 4/296-297.

[36] Ibid 4/297.

[37] *Madaarijus Saalikeen* 2/294.

"Certainly fear of Allah, being conscious of Him and being dedicated to one's lofty purpose are the foundations for all of the excellent characteristics and manners that one should possess. [38]

Ibn Miskawaih gave the following definition for *Khuluq* (character and manners):

"It is a situation of the soul that calls it to perform certain deeds without any thought or pondering. This situation can be divided into two parts: one part is that which is naturally in a person from the time of his creation, like the person who becomes angry at the slightest provocation. Another part is that which is achieved through customary performance and practice. At first, it might be with pondering and thought but the person continues those acts until they become part of his being and nature. [39]

Al-Hasan said:

"Good manners entail generosity, giving charity and bearing mistakes committed by others. [40]

Ash-Sha'bi also said about good manners:

"Good manners entail (among other things): giving gifts generously and being graceful and cheerful (with the people) when one meets them." [41]

---

[38] *Al-Fawaa'id*, page 210.
[39] *Al-Mas'ooliyah Al-Khuluqiyyah wa Al-Jazaa' Alaiha*, page 17.
[40] *Jaami'ul Uloom wal-Hikam*, page 457.
[41] Ibid.

Salaam Ibn Abi Mutai was asked about good manners and he replied in poetry saying:

> *"You see him smiling when you come to him, as if you are giving him what you are asking him to give you! If he has nothing in his hands save his soul, he will give it. So whoever asks him should show piety. He is just like the sea which you can reach from any direction. Goodness is its waves and generosity is its beach."* [42]

Imam Ahmed said:

> *"Good manners mean that you should neither get angry nor nervous."*

He also said: *"Good manners entail bearing others faults."* [43]

I ask Allah the Exalted to accept this from me and to make it be of great benefit to the reader as surely the reminder benefits.

---

[42] *Ad-Dewaan* p113 *Bi Sharh Tha-labah*
[43] *Jaami ul Uloom wal Hikam* p457

Allah the Exalted says in the Quran:

وَإِنَّكَ لَعَلَىٰ خُلُقٍ عَظِيمٍ

"And verily, you (O Muhammad) are on an exalted standard of character." (Al-Qalam 4)

Allah also says:

وَٱلۡكَـٰظِمِينَ ٱلۡغَيۡظَ وَٱلۡعَافِينَ عَنِ ٱلنَّاسِ ۗ وَٱللَّهُ يُحِبُّ ٱلۡمُحۡسِنِينَ

"Who repress anger and who pardon men; verily, Allah loves *Al-Muhsinoon* (the good-doers)." (Aali Imraan 134)

[Hadith 621]

Anas ﷺ reported:

كَانَ رَسُولُ اللهِ صَلَّى اللهُ عَلَيْهِ وسَلَّم أَحْسَنَ النَّاسِ خُلقاً. متفقٌ عليه.

"The Messenger of Allah ﷺ was the best of all the people in behavior." [Agreed upon]

[EXPLANATION OF OPENING VERSES AND HADITH 621]

The author Imam An-Nawawi ﷾ presents this chapter pertaining to good manners; and what is intended by this is to encourage, urge and motivate one towards good conduct and behavior and shedding light on its lofty status and how an individual may obtain it. So, good conduct can be divided into the following two categories:

1. One's conduct with Allah
2. One's conduct with the people

Regarding good conduct with Allah then it is: accepting and being pleased with Allah's Decree's and Legislations, and submitting to them with full acceptance without any signs of discontent, displeasure, ill-feelings or sadness. So, if Allah the Exalted afflicts one of His slaves, this individual completely acknowledges that this trail, misfortune or disliked matter is from none other than Allah, so he (or she) endures it patiently and acknowledges in his heart and confesses with his tongue, "I am pleased with Allah as My Lord." All-in-all, whatsoever Allah ordains for him he willingly accepts and submits to his fate, has patience, obeys and follows the legislations of Islam as well as also submitting to it and being fully content within himself, this is considered good manners with Allah ﷻ.

As for good conduct with the people then it is as some of the *Ulama* have said:

1. Refraining from harming others
2. Being generous
3. Having a cheerful friendly smiling face

As for the first of these three: refraining from harming others, then this means that one does not harm others, not by word, statement or action.

As for being generous: then this means he gives generously whatever he has, be it wealth or he propagates knowledge or the likes of what is considered an act of generosity.

And lastly, having a cheerful friendly smiling face. This means meeting people in the most graceful and pleasing charming manner other than having a gloomy face, or turning one's cheek away from the people in a dishonorable way. So, this is considered good manners with the creation or the people.

There is no doubt that the one who does as we have just said, certainly he (or she) will endure patiently any harm he encounters from others, for sure if one is greatly harmed by others and is as we said, patient, verily this is counted and considered as good manners for sure. This is because man will surely face many obstacles and ill treatment from either his brethren or the likes and this could be by way of them transgressing against him, either taking his wealth or denying him his rights or the likes; if this wronged individual endures such harms and is patient hoping in Allah's great reward for enduring them, certainly the good ending is for the righteous. So, the author begins this chapter with the following statement of Allah the Exalted and High when He says in the Quran:

نٓ ۚ وَٱلْقَلَمِ وَمَا يَسْطُرُونَ • مَآ أَنتَ بِنِعْمَةِ رَبِّكَ بِمَجْنُونٍ • وَإِنَّ لَكَ لَأَجْرًا غَيْرَ مَمْنُونٍ • وَإِنَّكَ لَعَلَىٰ خُلُقٍ عَظِيمٍ

"Noon [These letters (*Noon,* etc.) are one of the miracles of the Quran, and none but Allah (Alone) knows their meanings]. By the pen and what the (Angels) write (in the records of men); you (O Muhammad) are not, by the grace of your Lord, a madman, and verily, you (O Muhammad) are on an exalted standard of character." (Al-Qalam 1-4)

The meaning of **And verily, you..."** is referring to Prophet Muhammad ﷺ, and as for Allah's Words: **"And verily, you (O Muhammad) are on an exalted standard of Character,"** Allah also states this about Prophet Muhammad ﷺ; what is meant by this is, that no one was equal in match with him in all matters, such as, in his conduct and manners with Allah, his honorable conduct and manners with the people and how brave he was, how generous he was, how he handled and dealt with matters, and generally how he was. His manners were the Quran, meaning, he behaved as the Quran calls one to behave, and what is again meant by this is, whenever He was told by Allah to do such-and-such, he would comply to these commands right away and whenever the Quran told him to stay away from such-and-such forbidden matter he would refrain instantly and avoid such prohibited matters. So, the author mentions the next verse where Allah says:

وَٱلْكَـٰظِمِينَ ٱلْغَيْظَ وَٱلْعَافِينَ عَنِ ٱلنَّاسِ ۗ وَٱللَّهُ يُحِبُّ ٱلْمُحْسِنِينَ

"Who repress anger and who pardon men; verily, Allah loves *Al-Muhsinoon* (the good-doers)." (Aali Imraan 134)

144

This verse is a description and characteristic of the God-fearing believer that Allah has prepared Paradise for, as He says in the Quran in this same verse mentioned but just before it:

۞ وَسَارِعُوٓاْ إِلَىٰ مَغْفِرَةٍ مِّن رَّبِّكُمْ وَجَنَّةٍ عَرْضُهَا ٱلسَّمَٰوَٰتُ وَٱلْأَرْضُ أُعِدَّتْ لِلْمُتَّقِينَ ۞ ٱلَّذِينَ يُنفِقُونَ فِى ٱلسَّرَّآءِ وَٱلضَّرَّآءِ وَٱلْكَٰظِمِينَ ٱلْغَيْظَ وَٱلْعَافِينَ عَنِ ٱلنَّاسِ ۗ وَٱللَّهُ يُحِبُّ ٱلْمُحْسِنِينَ

"And be quick for forgiveness from your Lord, and for a Paradise as wide as are the heavens and the earth, prepared for *Al-Muttaqoon*, (the pious), those who spend [in Allah's Cause – by deeds of charity, alms etc.], in prosperity and in adversity, who repress anger and who pardon men; verily, Allah loves *Al-Muhsinoon* (the good-doers)." (Aali Imraan 133-134)

So, Allah says: **"who repress anger,"** which means, those who restrain, subdue and withhold their anger whenever they become angry, they control themselves and do not make this anger and rage they feel transgress against anyone. So, Allah next says:

"And who pardon men," Meaning, if anyone wrongs or ill-treats them. Then Allah says: **"Verily, Allah loves *Al-Muhsinoon* (the good-doers)."** Because, good treatment is, if anyone wrongs you, you forgive them, but in saying this, this has conditions! If this wrong doer is of those deserving forgiveness them it is highly recommended to forgive them, but if it is the opposite and they are not of those deserving your forgiveness then it is looked down upon to grant them such forgiveness, as Allah the Exalted says:

وَجَزَٰٓؤُا۟ سَيِّئَةٍ سَيِّئَةٌ مِّثْلُهَا ۖ فَمَنْ عَفَا وَأَصْلَحَ فَأَجْرُهُۥ عَلَى ٱللَّهِ ۚ إِنَّهُۥ لَا يُحِبُّ ٱلظَّٰلِمِينَ

"But whoever forgives and makes reconciliation, his reward is due from Allah." (Al-Shura 40)

So, if someone wrongs you, hits or insults you or the likes, should you forgive such an individual or not? We say, the matter needs some clarity! If this wrongdoer is an evil-minded evildoer, then if you forgive him (or her) this will only make him increase in his wrongdoing to you or to another person, in this case no, he should not be forgiven rather, one should request one's God-given rights.

And if the matter is of those matters that can be referred to those in authority, then one should refer the matter to them, but like we said, if that is not the case and one is able to demand one's right directly himself, then he should request them but with a condition, and that condition is that in demanding such rights it does not lead to greater harm as an outcome. So Allah says:

"But whoever forgives and makes reconciliation": Forgiving (such wrongdoers) when absolutely no reconciliation is made, we say in that case, demand your right but if this individaul is generally not as we have described (a wicked person), then forgiveness in recommended.

[Hadith 622]

Anas ﷺ reported:

مَا مَسِسْتُ دِيباجاً ولاَ حَرِيراً أَلْيَنَ مِنْ كَفِّ رسُولِ اللهِ صَلَّى اللهُ عَلَيْهِ وسَلَّم ، وَلاَ
شَمَمْتُ رائِحَةً قَطُّ أَطْيَبَ مِن رَسُولِ اللهِ صَلَّى اللهُ عَلَيْهِ وسَلَّم ، وَلَقَدْ خَدَمْتُ
رَسُولَ اللهِ صَلَّى اللهُ عَلَيْهِ وسَلَّم عشْرَ سِنِينَ ، فَما قالَ لِي قَطُّ : أُفِّ ، وَلا قالَ
لِشَيْءٍ فَعَلْتُهُ : لِمَ فَعَلْتَهُ؟ ولا لشيءٍ لَمْ افْعَلْهُ : أَلاَ فَعَلْتَ كَذا؟ متفقٌ عليه .

"I never felt any piece of velvet or silk softer than the palm of the
Messenger of Allah ﷺ, nor did I smell any fragrance more
pleasant than the smell of the Messenger of Allah. I served him
for ten years, and He never said 'Uff (an expression of disgust)
to me. He never said 'Why did you do that?' for something I had
done, nor did he ever say, 'Why did you not do such-and-such,'
for something I had not done." [Agreed upon]

[Hadith 623]

Sa'b Ibn Jaththamah ﷺ reported:

أَهْدَيْتُ رسُولَ اللهِ صَلَّى اللهُ عَلَيْهِ وسَلَّم حِمَاراً وَحْشِياً ، فَرَدُّهُ عليَّ ، فلمّا رأَى مَا
في وَجْهي قالَ:«إِنَّا لَمْ نَرُدَّهُ عَلَيْكَ إِلاَّ لأَنَّا حُرُمٌ » متفقٌ عليه .

"I presented a wild ass to the Messenger of Allah ﷺ as a gift but
he returned it to me. When he precieved signs of despair on my
face, he said: 'I have declined to accept it because I am in the
state of Ihraam.'" [Agreed upon]

[EXPLANATION OF HADITH 622]

So, the author firstly mentions a narration of Anas Ibn Maalik ☙. When the Prophet ﷺ came to *Al-Madinah,* Anas's mother came to the Prophet ﷺ and gave Anas ☙ to him and said "This is Anas, and I willing give him to you to serve you." So the Prophet ﷺ excepted Anas ☙ gracefully and he would help and serve the Prophet ﷺ. So after that the Prophet ﷺ made *Dua* (supplication) for Anas ☙ that Allah bless him in his wealth and offspring, and certainly Allah enriched and blessed Anas ☙ to the point that he had a garden which produced fruit twice a year. This was all because of the Prophet's ﷺ *Dua* to Allah for Anas ☙ to be blessed; similarly, with respect to his offspring, his children reached over one hundred and twenty. Again, this was due to the Prophet's ﷺ blessed supplication for him.

Anas's ☙ statement regarding the Prophet's ﷺ hand, that it was softer than velvet and silk – then just as Allah the Exalted softened his hands He also softened and made his heart similar as the Exalted says in the Quran:

$$فَبِمَا رَحْمَةٍ مِّنَ ٱللَّهِ لِنتَ لَهُمْ$$

"And by the Mercy of Allah, you dealt with them (the believers) gently."

Meaning: you were very kind and gently towards them, and Allah goes on to say in the same verse:

وَلَوْ كُنتَ فَظًّا غَلِيظَ ٱلْقَلْبِ لَانفَضُّواْ مِنْ حَوْلِكَ ۖ فَٱعْفُ عَنْهُمْ
وَٱسْتَغْفِرْ لَهُمْ وَشَاوِرْهُمْ فِى ٱلْأَمْرِ ۖ فَإِذَا عَزَمْتَ فَتَوَكَّلْ عَلَى ٱللَّهِ

"And by the Mercy of Allah, you dealt with them
gently, and had you been severe and harsh-hearted,
they would have broken away from about you; so
pass over (their faults), and ask (Allah's) forgiveness
for them; and consult them in the affair; then when
you have taken a decision, put your trust in Allah."
(Aali Imraan 159)

Likewise, regarding the Prophet's ﷺ smell, Anas ؓ said: "Nor
did I smell any fragrance more pleasant than the smell of the
Messenger of Allah ﷺ." And this was due to the Prophet's ﷺ
frequent habit of using plenty of perfume, and he (the Prophet
ﷺ) said regarding perfume:

*"Made beloved to me from your Dunyah (life of this world)
is women, perfume and the prayer has been made a cooler
to my eye."*

It is known that the Prophet ﷺ was good and so was every
thing about him - to the point that his Companions uset to
hasten to collect his sweat due to it being honourable and a
pleasent smell, and they used to obtain blessings from it, and
this was a special feature specifically only for the Prophet ﷺ, as
well as his saliva and his clothes which also contained blessing
in them, but as for anyone other than the Prophet ﷺ, then one
does not seek blessings from their sweat or saliva as this was
only something specific for the Prophet ﷺ.

Anas ﷺ further said: "I served Him for ten years, and He never said '*Uff*'"; meaning: the Prophet ﷺ never got annoyed or upset with me ever in all the ten years time that I served him. Certainly, as we know, if we have a servant or the likes or even a companion serving us, lets say for just a week or around that time, we will find some fault in him for sure or become annoyed with him at least! But, not so with the Prophet ﷺ, as Anas ﷺ remained with him for a total of ten years!

Anas ﷺ said: "He never said '*Uff*' (an expression of disgust) to me. He never said 'Why did you do that?' for something I had done, nor did he ever say, 'Why did you not do such-and-such,' for something I had not done." So, even when Anas ﷺ used his own personal opinion in matters, even then then the Prophet ﷺ never rebuked or scorned him or chastised him, bearing in mind that Anas ﷺ served him daily! So all of this is a clear indication that the Prophet ﷺ clearly conformed with the statement of Allah when He said in the Quran:

$$ خُذِ ٱلْعَفْوَ وَأْمُرْ بِٱلْعُرْفِ وَأَعْرِضْ عَنِ ٱلْجَٰهِلِينَ $$

"Show forgiveness, enjoin what is good, and turn away from the foolish." (Al-A'raaf 199)

So dear reader! Do you know what forgiveness means? It is to be forgiving towards the people whenever you encounter ills from them and to simplify matters for people, and that is that you do not expect from them perfection in all matters in life. And we say, if a person excepts perfection all the time from the people, for sure, he will be let down and disappointed very much. So make things easy for the people and try not to become angry with them and overlook their short comings and thier faults as Anas ﷺ said: "He never said 'Why did you do that?' for something I had done, nor did he ever say, 'Why did you not do such-and-such,' for something I had not done." This shows us the perfect conduct and outstanding manners of the Prophet ﷺ.

[EXPLANATION OF HADITH 623]

From the noble conduct of the Prophet ﷺ was that he never hid his intentions, rather he aways revealed them towards anyone in the religion. And He never made even a moment go by except that that was to thier advantage. So, Sa'b Ibn Jaththamah was known to be an unbeaten archer, so he happened to be with the Prophet ﷺ when he was in the state of *Ihraam*, so one day the Prophet ﷺ went to visit him and Sa'b was blessed to have the best guest he could ever have, so he went out and hunted a wild-ass for the Prophet ﷺ, and as is well known, these type of animals were easily available in the Arabia peninsula and were more available than other hunting animals; so Sa'b gave this wild-ass to the Prophet ﷺ but he declined it and returned it, so Sa'b was somewhat unhappy about this. And he wondered why the Prophet ﷺ had returned his gift, so his face expressed signs of grief, so when the Prophet ﷺ noticed this from him he said: "I have declined to accept it because I am in the state of Ihraam" [44]

---

[44] *Ihraam* (a state or ritual consecration during *Hajj* or *Ummrah*) is the first of the rites of *Hajj,* and it refers to the intention to start the rites. It is called *Ihraam* (which is derived from the Arabic word "*Haraam,*" i.e. forbidden) because a pilgrim by assuming *Ihraam* prohibits himself from

And as is well known, it is not allowed for someone to hunt game for the one in the state of *Ihraam*. So, if a person happens to be in the state of *Ihraam* and you are in your own counrty and he visits you, and you hunt for him some game or sacrifice an animal for him, whatever it may be from things which are hunted, it is unlawful for him to eat from that, as he is the state for *Ihraam*, but on the other hand, if this game was

---

certain acts that were permissible before being in that state, such as sexual intercourse, wearing perfume, clipping one's finger nails, having one's hair cut, or wearing certain kinds of clothes.

Regarding hunting in the state of *Ihraam*, Shaykh Fowzaan stated: There are nine prohibated actions one is forbidden to do in the state of *Ihraam*....."(the ninth): It is forbidden for one in the state of *Ihraam* to kill game animals as Allah the Exalted says in the Quran: **"O you who believe! Kill not game while you are in the state of *Ihraam*."** (Al- Maa'idah 95)

That is, do not kill game animals while being in the state of *Ihraam* to perform *Hajj* or *Umrah* also Allah says: **"Forbidden to you is game from the land as long as you are in the state of *Ihraam*."** (Al-Maa'idah 96)

That is to say, those in a state of *Ihraam* are forbidden to hunt or kill game animals, or help in hunting or slaughtering them. Likewise, it is prohibited for a *Muhrim* (the one in the state of *Ihraam*) to eat game animal which he hunted, which was hunted for him, or which he helped in hunting, as it will be regarded as a dead animal in this case, which is unlawful to eat. Still, it is not prohibited for a *Muhrim* to eat fish or animals from the sea, whether he hunts it or anyone else does it for him, as Allah the Exalted says: **"Lawful to you is game from the sea and its food."** (Al-Maa'idah 96)

On the other hand, it is permissible for a *Muhrim* to slaughter a domestic animal such as a chicken, sheep, and cattle, as they are not game animals. A *Muhrim* is also permitted to kill wild inedible animals, such as lions, and tigers for such creatures threaten people's lives. See *Al-Mulakhas ul-Fiqh,* p270 by Shaykh Saalih Fowzaan.

not hunted spefically for him, in that case in would be lawful for him to eat.

In another *Hadith* when Abu Qataadah ﷺ presented to the Prophet ﷺ something he himself had hunted, but was not hunted for a sole purpose of the Prophet ﷺ, the Prophet ate from that hunted game, and this is the most correct view related to this issue. What we mean is, if a person hunts any prey for his own sake or soley for his own self and the one in the state of *Ihraam* eats from that hunt this would be allowed as it was not hunted for him.

So, regarding this issue some of the Scholars have said: it is completely unlawful for anyone in the state of *Ihraam* to eat any form of hunted animal, whether it was hunted for the one in the state of *Ihraam* or not hunted for him (maybe it was hunted soley for themself), so in both cases, they say it is completely forbidden. And they say, the *Hadith* of Sa'b Ibn Jaththamah occurred after the *Hadith* of Abu Qataadah, and that the *Hadith* of Abu Qataadah was in the sixth year after *Hijrah* (i.e. the sixth year after the Prophet ﷺ entered *Al-Madinah*), and the *Hadith* of Sa'b Ibn Jaththamah occurred in the tenth year after the Prophet ﷺ entered *Al-Madinah*, so Sa'b's *Hadith* was later and is given precedence over Abu Qataadah's *Hadith*, but this is wrong! Why? Because this would mean that Sa'b Ibn Jaththamah's *Hadith* abrogates Abu Qataadah's *Hadith*, and the fundamental *Hadith* principle states, "If reconcilliation cannot be made between two conflicting texts, then one is considered abrogated." But, it is possible in this case to make reconcilliation, this is surely possible, and that reconcillition is made by saying that if this hunted game was hunted specifically for the one in the state of

Ihraam then it is unlawful for him (or her) to eat. But on the other hand if it was not, then it is as we said, lawful for him to eat this game; so if another person hunts this game for himself then the one in the state of *Ihraam* may eat himself from that game. And that which supports this, is the *Hadith* of Jaabir Ibn Abdullah who said the Prophet ﷺ said:

> *"The eating of game is lawful for you in the state of Ihraam provided you yourselves do not kill it or it was killed for you by someone else."*[45]

In this *Hadith* there are two great benefits:

1. The Prophet ﷺ never hid his true intentions, rather he aways revealed them towards anyone in the religion, and had it not been for the fact that he was in the state of *Ihraam,* he would have accepted Sa'b's gift; he remained silent so as to make Sa'b question him as to why he refused his gift, so that Sa'b would not become upset at his refusal of his gift and so that the Prophet ﷺ could explain himself.

2. One should aways explain himself in matters that are at times not clear so that the person you are dealing with, be it in any matter, would not have bad thoughts or ideas in his mind about the matter or about you.

---

[45] *Abu Dawood Ahmed At-Tirmidi* and *Mishkaat,* Shaykh Al-Albaani says this *Hadith* is *Da'if* (weak narration); see his *Sunan At-Tirmidi* 846 and also he says it is *Da'if* in *Sunan Abi Dawood* 1851; he considers it *Da'if* in *Sunan An-Nisaa-i* 2827. Shaykh Al-Albaani says the reason why this *Hadith* is weak is because Abu Abdir Rahmaan said, in the chain of this *Hadith* is Amir Ibn Abi Amir, and he not strong in *Hadith* even thought Maalik would narrate from him; see his *Sunan Al-Nisaa'i* 2827 (Published by Makatabat ul-Ma'aarif).

And this is so that you make the people feel comfortable around you as well as them having a sound state of mind, as surely this is from the fine lofty manners and guidance of the Prophet Muhammad ﷺ.

[Hadith 624]

Nawwaas Ibn Sam'aan ﷺ reported: I asked the Messenger of Allah
ﷺ about virtue and sin and he said:

«البِرُّ حُسنُ الخُلُقِ، والإِثمُ: ما حاكَ في نَفسِكَ، وكَرِهتَ أَن يَطَّلِعَ عَلَيهِ النّاسُ » رواهُ
مسلم.

*"Virtue is noble behaviour, and sin is that which creates doubt
and you do not like people to know about it."* [Reported by
Muslim]

[Hadith 625]

Abdullah Ibn Amr Ibn Al-Aas ﷺ reported:

لم يكن رسولُ اللهِ صَلَّى اللهُ عَلَيهِ وسَلَّم فاحِشاً ولا مُتَفَحِّشاً. وكانَ يَقُولُ : « إِنَّ
مِن خِيارِكُم أَحسَنَكُم أَخلاقاً » متفقٌ عليه.

*"The Messenger of Allah ﷺ did not indulge in vain talk nor did
he like to listen to it. He used to say: 'The best of you is the best
you in conduct.'"* [Agreed upon]

[Hadith 626]

Abu ad-Darda ﷺ reported the Prophet ﷺ said:

« ما مِن شَيءٍ أَثقَلُ في مِيزانِ المؤمِنِ يَومَ القِيامةِ مِن حُسنِ الخُلُقِ . وإِنَّ اللهَ
يُبغِضُ الفاحِشَ البَذيِّ» رواه الترمذي وقال : حديث حسن صحيح .

*"Nothing will be heavier on the Day of Resurrection in the scales of the
believer than good manners. Allah hates one who utters foul or coarse
language."* [Reported by At-Tirmidhi]

[EXPLANATION OF HADITH 624, 625 AND 626]

The author (Imam An-Nawawi) mentions these *Ahaadith* pertaining to good manners, so as for the first of them, then it is that of Nawwaas Ibn Sam'aan ☺ who said: "I asked Messenger of Allah ﷺ about virtue and sin and he said: *'Virtue is noble behaviour.'*"

So, regarding good manners then we have previously explained it, and in short we said it is a trait that if an individual actualizes, for certain he (or she) will obtain plenty of good. As for the word "Virtue," then it means plenty of good. And as for the word: "Sin," then the Prophet ﷺ said it is *"that which creates doubt and you do not like people to know about it."* This means: that this wrong is unsettling within a person, and it leaves one in a confusing state, indecisive, hesitant, and wavering. So, this narration is addressing none other than an upright God-fearing person, but as for the immoral sinner, then this is not the case, as wrongdoing does not alter his (or her) state as the sinful one has little conscience or feelings of guilt as to what he does, and he cares very little if at all as to what people will say or think of him if they see him openly disobeying Allah.

But the person who fears Allah, then Allah puts light in his heart, so whenever he does wrong or commits a sin, this bothers him greatly, as well as leaving him unsettled about this wrong he is embarking upon and he very much dislikes anyone to glance at him in the act of sin. So, this is the gage between the righteous and the sinner. And as for those who care very little if people see them disobeying Allah, they feel little or no remorse whatsoever about their wrong doings, so their hearts pain them not in the least whether they sin or whether people see them sinning, rather they, and we seek refuge in Allah, seem to be delighted and joyful when they embark upon a sinful path! Allah ﷻ says in the Quran:

أَفَمَن زُيِّنَ لَهُۥ سُوٓءُ عَمَلِهِۦ فَرَءَاهُ حَسَنًا ۖ فَإِنَّ ٱللَّهَ يُضِلُّ مَن يَشَآءُ

وَيَهْدِى مَن يَشَآءُ ۖ فَلَا تَذْهَبْ نَفْسُكَ عَلَيْهِمْ حَسَرَٰتٍ ۚ إِنَّ ٱللَّهَ عَلِيمٌۢ

بِمَا يَصْنَعُونَ

"Is he, to whom the evil of his deeds are made fair-seeming so that he considers it as good (equal to one who is rightly-guided)? Verily, Allah sends astray whom He wills and guides whom He wills." (Al-Faatir 8)

So, the person's evil deed becomes fair-seeming to him and he becomes gladdened by such wicked and vile deeds; for example, you see a habitual drinker overly cheerful in his heart when he is drinking this alcohol, as well as those who indulge in *Riba* (usury or interest), fornication and prostitution, they seem quite content and pleased in doing these vile evil actions; in-fact many seem so happy doing these evil degrading acts that they make them known and feel quite lax propogating such immoralities wherever thier feet take them. And at times when they travel to shameless sinful countries, when they return from these places they boast openly about what they have indulged in from such acts such as fornication, the drinking of intoxicants and the likes, and Allah's refuge is sought!

In these many narraions is a proof for the following: the indictation of the Prophet's ﷺ outstanding sublime attributes and that is that he did not indulge in loose talk nor did he like to listen to it. And this means he was far from obsene indecent foul speech, rather he was honourable and had a dignified personality, and was simply easy going and quite gentle and far from the use of vulgar filthy shameful language; he was the farthest from using these dirty obsene words verbally, nor did he behave in any obscene way towards anyone.

And also from the benefits of these narrations is the encouragement towards good manners and good conduct, and this is due to the fact that good manners are counted among those things on the Day of Rescurrection that are the heaviest things on a person's scales, and this chapter is a great encouragement and awaking. So dear brothers (and sisters), do your best to behave towards Allah the Exalted in the best manner you are able to, and submit to His leglislated Devine Law and Decree, and do this with full acceptance with a submissive obedient heart as well as exibiting the most refined manners and character towards your fellow brethen for indeed Allah the Exalted loves the doers of good.

[Hadith 627]

Abu Hurairah ﷺ reported:

« تَقْوَى اللَّهِ وَحُسْنُ الخُلُقِ وَسُئِلَ عن أَكْثَرِ مَا يُدْخِلُ النَّاسَ النَّارَ فَقَالَ: « الفَمُ
وَالفَرْجُ ». رواه الترمذي وقال: حديث حسن صحيح

*The Messenger of Allah ﷺ was asked about the deed which will
be foremost in leading a man to Paradise, He replied: "Fear of
Allah and good conduct." Then he was asked about indulgence
which will lead a man to Hell and he answered: "The tongue
and the private parts." [Reported by At-Tirmidhi]*

[Hadith 628]

Abu Hurairah ﷺ reported that the Messenger ﷺ said:

« أَكْمَلُ المُؤْمِنِينَ إِيمَاناً أَحْسَنُهُم خُلُقاً، وخِيَارُكُم خِيَارُكُمْ لِنِسَائِهِمْ » رواه الترمذي

*"The most perfect man in his faith among the believers is the one
whose behaviour is most excellent; and the best of you are those
who are best to their wives." [Reported by At-Tirmidhi]*

160

[EXPLANATION OF HADITH 627 AND 628]

These *Ahaadith* highlight the great virtue of good conduct and from them is the *Hadith* of Abu Hurairah ﷺ that the Prophet ﷺ was asked about the deed which will be foremost in leading a man to Paradise, so he replied: *"Fear of Allah and good conduct."* The word *Taqwah* (piety and fear of Allah) consists of the following:

1. Obeying the commandments of Allah.
2. Staying away from what He has forbidden.

So, implementing what Allah the Exalted has commanded and refraining from what He has forbidden is defined as *Taqwah*, and this word is a noun derived from the root word: *"Al-Wiqaayah"* which means, "to protect." So *Taqwah* means: "to protect oneself from Allah's anger and punishment." One protects himself from Allah's punishment by performing what Allah has commanded and refraining from what He has prohibited. So, as for when the Prophet ﷺ was asked about indulgence which would lead a man to Hell, he ﷺ answered: *"The tongue and the private parts."*

As for the tongue, and why it is a cause for an individual entering Hell because of it, then it is because of a statement that a person utters giving it no consideration whatsoever and by that he is thrown in to the Fire the distance of seventy years, So for this reason the Prophet ﷺ said to Mu'adh Ibn Jabal ﷺ:

> *"Shall I tell you of that which holds all these things?"* I said, "Yes, O Messenger of Allah!" So he took hold of his tongue and said, *"Keep this in control."* I asked: O

Messenger of Allah! Shall we really be held to account for what we talk about?" He replied, *"May your mother lose you! People will be thrown on their faces into to the Hell on account of their tongues!"*

So, due to the fact that most of what people say is said with no consideration or thought given, a person rarely reflects what he (or she) utters, the matter has become regarding the tongue a light matter! Why? The reason why the tongue is not like a person's hands or eyes, is because ones hands and eyes become tired due to working and the likes, not so the tongue (ones speech), one can go on talking almost forever non-stop never even having a moment to pause or the slightest break.

So, you see a person constantly chatting about matters that are of little benefit, if any at all, mostly harmful things such backbiting, tale-bearing, swearing, cursing, abusing and insulting others, giving none of this even a slightest thought or even a moment's consideration!

As for the private parts, then this refers to fornication, homosexuality being the worst kind, and for sure a person's desires constantly calls him (or her) to indulge in such matters! And it goes without saying, this is especially the case with respect to the youth. And these types of things do not occur over one night, and what we mean is, one's desires gradually incite him or her towards fornication, whether person perceives it not. For this reason the Prophet ﷺ made clear every avenue to block the pathways leading one to fall prey to every form of indecent vile act of immorality.

For example, he ﷺ forbid a man to remain alone with an unrelated woman, and also he forbid a woman to expose her face in front of unrelated strange men and he forbid a woman to beautify her voice so as to provoke the one who has a sickness in his heart who might be moved by her seductive voice. So the Prophet ﷺ laid down many preventative measures against such detested immoralities so as to safeguard people from falling into these many vices that this *Hadith* is drawing one's intention to, and to be on guard against such things and to preserve and safeguard ones private parts from falling into the forbidden as well as highlighting the greatest causes that one could enter the Fire due to.

The next *Hadith* also highlights the virtue of excellence good manners, and that the best of people are those who have the best manners and they are those who have the most complete *Emaan* (faith), so the Prophet ﷺ said: *"The most perfect man in his faith among the believers is the one whose behaviour is most excellent."*

In this hadith is the following benefit: it is a proof and an indication that *Emaan* (faith) is of different levels, and that some peoples' *Emaan* is more complete and stronger than that of others, and the reason? The reason is, that it is due to their actions, so the more better an individual's conduct and manners are complete, then the higher his *Emaan* will be. This *Hadith* makes that clear, so it is biding upon you to exhibit fine character, manners and conduct to the best of your capability.

Lastly the Prophet said: *"And the best of you are those who are best to their wives."* And what is intended here is, the best of you are those who are the best to their wives and this is backed up by another statement of the Prophet ﷺ when he said: *"The best of you are those who are best to their family, and I am the best of you toward my family."*

So know that it is upon those married with families to behave towards them in the most excellent and outstanding caring loving affectionate way. Why? The reason why, is because that's what they are entitled to! One's family is the most deserving of all people to good treatment, rather the best treatment, and as we know those closest to us are those most entitled to be given precedence to this honorable treatment.

And with great regret, there are some people today who display the best manners toward other people and those around them but, when it comes to their own families they are the worst of all people toward them in their dealing with them and we seek Allah's refuge! And for sure this clearly goes against the way the Prophet 🌸 was as well as how he taught a man how he should behave toward his own family. What is worth mentioning here is, what is correct is that one should do his upmost to be balanced between the two and that is, he should be good and honorable and well-mannered with the people and at the same time, and on the same footing, with his family, both equal in good treatment but deal with his family with the best manners he possibly ever could. So do not forget your family always comes first, and they never should be forgotten, and they are most deserving of good treatment before the people.

So, when A'ishah 🌸 was asked how the Prophet 🌸 was at home, she said he used to be in the service of his family, and what she meant was that He would help his family in matters in the home, he would milk the sheep for his family, mend his own sandals and sew his own cloths. So in short this is how a person should behave with his family, so that they can be the closest and become the dearest of people to him.

[Hadith 629]

A'ishah ⁣﷞ reported: I heard the Messenger of Allah ﷺ saying:

« إِنَّ الْمُؤْمِنَ لَيُدْرِكُ بِحُسنِ خُلُقِه دَرَجةَ الصائِمِ القَائِمِ» رواه أبو داود.

"A believer will attain by his good behaviour the rank of the one who prays during the night and observes fasting during the day."
[Reported by Abu Dawud]

[Hadith 630]

Abu Umaamah Al-Bahili ⁣﷠ reported that the Messenger ﷺ said:

« أَنا زَعِيمٌ بِبَيتٍ في رَبَضِ الجنَّةِ لِمَنْ تَرَكَ المِراءَ . وَإِنْ كَانَ مُحِقّاً ، وَبِبيتٍ في وَسَطِ الجنَّةِ لِمَنْ تَرَكَ الكَذِبَ ، وإِن كَانَ مازِحاً ، وَبِبيتٍ في أَعلى الجنَّةِ لِمَن حَسُنَ خُلُقُهُ » حديث صحيح ، رواه أبو داود بإسناد صحيح.

"I guarantee a house in Paradise for the one who gives up arguing even if he is in the right; and I guarantee a home in the middle of Paradise for one who abandons lying even for the sake of fun; and I guarantee a house in the highest part of Paradise for one who has good manners." *[Reported by Abu Dawud]*

[Hadith 631]

Jaabir ◉ reported the Messenger of Allah ◉ said:

« إِنَّ مِنْ أَحَبِّكُمْ إِلَيَّ، وَأَقْرَبِكُمْ مِنِّي مَجْلِساً يَوْمَ الْقِيَامَةِ، أَحَاسِنَكُمْ أَخْلاقاً. وَإِنَّ
أَبْغَضَكُمْ إِلَيَّ وَأَبْعَدَكُمْ مِنِّي يومَ الْقِيامةِ، الثَّرْثَارُونَ والْمُتَشَدِّقُونَ والْمُتَفَيْهِقُونَ» قالوا:
يا رسول الله قَدْ عَلِمْنَا الثَّرْثَارُونَ والْمُتَشَدِّقُونَ، فَمَا الْمُتَفَيْهِقُونَ؟ قال: « الْمُتَكَبِّرُونَ
». رواه الترمذي وقال: حديث حسن.

*"The dearest and nearest among you to me on the Day of
Resurresction will be one who is the best of you in manners; and
the most abhorent among you to me and the farthest of you from
me will be the pompous, the garrulous, and Al-Mutafihiqoon."
The Companions asked Him: "O Messenger of Allah! We know
about the pompous and the garrulous, but we do not know who
Al-Mutafihiqoon are?" He replied: "The arrogant people."
[Reported by At-Tirmidhi]*

166

[EXPLANATION OF HADITHS 629, 630 AND 631]

The author (Imam An-Nawawi) mentions these *Ahaadith* and from them is the Prophet's ﷺ statement regarding those who are the closest people to him on the Day of Resurrection, and they are the people best in manners. So know that the better you are in manners, the closer you will be to Allah and to the Prophet ﷺ; the farthest people from the Prophet ﷺ will be the pompous, the garrulous, and *Al-Mutafihiqoon* - the arrogant people. As for the word: "Pompous", this means a very talkative person, so whenever they are in a gathering they always dominate in talking over the people and do not let anyone speak other than them, and they seem to have the impression that only they are in that gathering and no one else, and that what others have to say is of little importance, and they dont want anyone else to talk; no doubt this is a type of pride as well as arrogance.

As for the word: *"Garrulous"*, this means, when the person talks he is loudmouthed, he presumes he is the most eloquent Arab in speech, so you find him speaking pure traditional Arabic among the general folk who hardly know classical Arabic, so they understand little of what he is saying; but in saying this, if you are teaching, then this should be done in pure classical Arabic as this well help your students to master Arabic, but as for the laymen who understand very little Arabic then it is not becoming to address them using it rather, you talk with them according to their dialect and this is so that they can understand you when you are addressing them and your words are not difficult upon them.

As for the word: *"Al-Mutafihiqoon"*, the Prophet ﷺ discribed them as arrogant people. It refers to one who has traits of ignorance, a person who considers himself above the people and he looks down upon the people. And when he walks he walks as if he is of great importance and might. And no doubt this is a totally dispraised characteristic as well as bad manners! And it is upon every individaul to distance himself (or herself) and be on guard from falling into this. So one most never forget his own worth, and that if Allah bestows upon a person wealth, knowledge, high standing or honour, it becomes biding upon him because of this to be very humble. As those who become humble due to Allah enriching them with these things, are in a better position than others who are humble due to natural reasons, so regarding haughtiness the Prophet ﷺ said, on the Day of Resurrection Allah will not talk nor look nor purify them and of them he said: *"A poor man who is proud."* Why? Why will Allah not talk nor look nor purify such an individaul? Because of what reason would a poor man be proud? What does he have that makes him haugty, after all he is poor, so why act in such a way!? So, this shows that pride is totally condemned. Like we said, those who are given knowledge, wealth and position, they are better when they act humble than other than them, and that is because they have a greater reason to a proud and they dont, when most people usually do. So, whoever Allah has bestowed upon from His Bounty should increase in gratitude and thankfulness toward Allah and increase in his submitting to the truth when it comes to him and be humble towards others, may Allah grant success to the Muslims and give them good manner and conduct and enable them to stay away from bad manners; indeed He is All-Generous All-Kind!